AT HOME
WITH PLANTS

AT HOME

Ian Drummond & Kara O'Reilly

WITH PLANTS

STYLING BY ELKIE BROWN
PHOTOGRAPHY BY NICK POPE

weldon**owen**

CONTENTS

THE HOUSEPLANT REVIVAL

There is no doubt that houseplants are once again having their moment. Though they were a popular feature of home decoration during the 1960s and 1970s, houseplants and plant prints fell out of favor when the minimalist 1990s hit. But today, with the revival of interest in craft skills, growing-your-own, and baking, people are embracing houseplants as another antidote to the increased demands of our tech-preoccupied world. With the return of a more eclectic, vibrant, individual approach to interior decorating, it was only a matter of time before the real plants that inspired the botanical fabrics and wallpapers of past decades were once again back in the spotlight.

In order to be a part of the houseplant revival, many of us need to overcome our fear—that sense that we have no idea how to look after plants. The good news is that, with a little bit of know-how, even the least green-thumbed among us can successfully grow an indoor plant—or two.

As well as a foolproof guide to houseplant care, this book is also a go-to resource for creative ideas on where to position and display them. Start small with, say, a cactus or a succulent, and once you've proven your plant-caring skills, we guarantee you

WHY REAL, NOT FAUX?

Given how far faux plants have come in their resemblance to the real thing, and the variety of fuss-free reproductions available, why choose the real thing? Because, let's face it, a faux is basically an ornament, whereas living plants evolve over time. A thriving plant is part of nature's rich cycle, and no amount of good fakery can replicate that. Bringing a part of nature into your home in the form of plants and nurturing them to give their best is hugely rewarding. What's more, they offer significant health benefits, too—but more on that later (see pages 14 and 137).

will want to introduce more into your home.

Ian and I are going to show our ages now, but we distinctly remember the role that plants played in the decoration of our childhood homes. From dramatic, glossy *Monstera deliciosa* (Swiss cheese plant) and *Ficus elastica* 'Decora' (rubber plant) in the living room to macramé-clad hanging *Chlorophytum comosum* (spider plant) in the kitchen, plants were embraced by our parents as decorative objects. With the advent of the yuppie 1980s, we, too, had the ubiquitous *Yucca elephantipes* (spineless yucca) in our teenage bedrooms. Like many others before us, we grew herbs in the kitchen and bulbs in window boxes in our first apartments. For me, this segued into the cactus years and the occasional purchase from East London's Columbia Road flower market—I still feel sad about the beautiful *Ficus benjamina* (weeping fig) that didn't survive when I moved apartments. Ian, meanwhile,

had the benefit of being able to bring home plant samples from work and became particularly fond of his *Spathiphyllum wallisii* (peace lily).

We have both observed the creeping return of greenery in the way some of the chicest folk around decorate their homes today. We have noticed cool interiors companies upping the variety of plant pots in their lines, and the resurgence of both terrariums and hanging planters as decorative elements in the design of cutting-edge boutique restaurants, shops, and cafés.

Now is the time to embrace this trend and run with it in your own home. With Ian's expertise at hand, we are hoping to help you break out of the safe zone of a supermarket basil plant that will wilt away like an afterthought in your kitchen. We hope to inspire, inform, and help you innovate with the way you use plants in your home. One of the most amazing things about houseplants is that you can enjoy them all year round, and there is really nothing more satisfying to the soul than nurturing a living thing.

Left:
This open terrarium is filled with a selection of small succulents and finished with some *Cladonia rangiferina* (reindeer moss), which is a type of lichen.

Above:
A collection of hardy succulents, cacti, and two bold *Sansevieria*—*S. bacularis* 'Mikado' and *S. cylindrica*—complement the dark wood of this modern sideboard.

TRENDS & AESTHETICS

The reemergence of the houseplant as a key feature in so many interior schemes has seriously gathered momentum over the last year or two. And the keen-eyed will have observed that the predominant design choice is evergreen plants.

Cacti and succulents are back in vogue, which can be put down to the popularity of terrariums as the preferred plant container among the cognoscenti. However, dramatic, large-scale plants, such as those 1970s favorites *Monstera deliciosa* (Swiss cheese plant), ferns, and *Fatsia japonica* (Japanese aralia), are also having their moment once again in the spotlight. Their aesthetic appeal in an interior lies in their bold shapes and potential impact. You just have to look at how top design companies such as Anthropologie and West Elm have used plants like these as the pattern inspiration for some of the coolest wallpaper and fabric prints around.

We can put all this down to the anti-minimalist backlash. After the pared-back, all-white, clean-line years, we have worked out that our homes are

BACK IN VOGUE

Once consigned to the style trash heap, the following stalwarts of 1970s houseplant schemes are seriously back in favor. They are all evergreen, with striking silhouettes and interesting leaf shapes, which means they will have an instant impact on an interior.

* *Aspidistra elatior* (cast-iron plant)
* *Asplenium nidus* (bird's nest fern)
* *Chlorophytum comosum* (spider plant)
* *Fatsia japonica* (Japanese aralia)
* *Ficus elastica* 'Decora' (rubber plant)
* *Monstera deliciosa* (Swiss cheese plant)
* *Sansevieria trifasciata* (mother-in-law's tongue)

actually our sanctuaries, not display homes in a real estate agent's brochure. Using color, pattern, and accent accessories is all about creating spaces that are truly personal to us. Plants fit well into this decorative approach, and if you look at them as pieces of living art that add extra layers of interest to your home, it becomes easier to know which ones to choose and where to put them.

Many of us also live in increasingly urbanized environments, with little or no access to outside space, so introducing houseplants into your home is the perfect way to reconnect with nature. You could even do as Ian does and treat them as members of the family—he goes so far as to give pet names to his favorites …

Technological advances in the way professional nurseries now propagate and grow plants mean they are much more affordable than they were, say, a decade ago. Nurseries in the Netherlands can produce literally millions of one variety of orchid, which makes the cost per plant around a quarter of what it was when orchids first emerged as a popular indoor plant a few years ago.

Affordable plants, combined with the easy availability of cool containers in stores and online, as well as simple yet inspirational ideas from the likes of Pinterest, Instagram, and the interiors of fashionable restaurants and shops, mean we can all attempt a planting scheme that suits our taste, our space, and our creative side.

THE NEXT BIG THING?

Following on from the hippy-chic good looks of macramé and other knotted or woven plant holders, *kokedama* is the latest creative way of displaying houseplants—without containers.

Kokedama, which translates to "moss ball," has its origins in Japan, where it is an offshoot of traditional bonsai (the art of deliberately stunting the growth of a tree or shrub for ornamental reasons), and it is already making its influence felt everywhere in the world of design and display. It involves removing a plant from its pot, shaking off the potting soil, then wrapping the root system in a kind of mud ball (made from a very particular mix of soil and specialty minerals and clays), before covering it with a layer of living moss tied in place with string.

Eye-catching? Definitely. High-maintenance? Yes, indeed. So, if it all sounds like too much hard work, you can always use a *Vanda* orchid, *Platycerium bifurcatum* (staghorn fern), or a few *Tillandsia* (air plant) instead to achieve the dramatic effect of a plant suspended in space.

Left:
Succulents, such as this *Echeveria*, are particularly appealing due to their architectural shape and interesting leaf colors— not to mention their indestructible qualities.

Above right:
That 1970s staple the *Chlorophytum comosum* (spider plant) is back in a big way. Display it in a hanging macramé planter for a nod to retro chic. It thrives in bathrooms and kitchens.

Colorful olive-storage tins at
UK emporium Rockett St George
lend themselves to some lovely
kitchen planting

Roots glass plant pot
by Istanbul-based design
company Nude Living

Succulents on show at hip
London hairdressers
Fourth Floor

Dramatic plants by Danish interior
design company Madam Stoltz (at
Out There Interiors in East Sussex)

Hanging planters by
Danish brand Bloomingville
(at Out There Interiors)

French designer Christian
Lacroix's plant-inspired
Soft Jardin Exo'Chic fabric
for Designers Guild

Palm Jungle wallpaper from
the Contemporary Restyled
collection by London-based
wallpaper designers Cole & Son

A plant cabinet by
Danish company Nordal
(at Out There Interiors)

The Tarovine wallpaper and fabric
print by London-based luxury
designers House of Hackney

Cacti styled by the design team
at London fashion and
interiors shop Darkroom

A bold lineup of indoor plants
at the restaurant Rawduck in
London Fields

Tiny terrariums by hip West
Sussex-based homeware e-tailers
Rockett St George

Glass herb vases by UK
interior design company
Cox & Cox

A *Philodendron xanadu* featured
in the "Paint by Conran"
lookbook from UK-based design
company The Conran Shop

A *Monstera deliciosa*
(Swiss cheese plant) in the
lookbook of London-based
interiors company Habitat

A collection of various
terrariums at UK interiors
emporium Graham & Green

Pillow featuring the
iconic Palmeral print
by House of Hackney

Contemporary ceramic
hanging planters by UK-based
e-boutique MiaFleur

THE PRACTICALITIES

HEALTH BENEFITS

You know that sense of well-being you get in spring when you walk by all the fresh, vibrant greens of new growth in parks and gardens, and even on city trees? With a couple of houseplants, you can experience that feeling year-round.

Connecting with nature and the natural world is just plain good for the soul. Given the fact that so many of us now spend more time indoors than ever before, chained to our laptops, it stands to reason that bringing some of the great outdoors into our interior spaces will have a positive effect on our sense of well-being. This is particularly relevant if you don't have immediate access to, or even a good view of, any green outdoor space.

There have been numerous studies on the health benefits of having plants in the workplace, so you can bet your bottom dollar they will have a positive effect in your home as well. Plants are, after all, Earth's oxygenators. The by-product of photosynthesis is oxygen, and there can be no harm in introducing a couple of natural oxygenators to your home environment.

While more specific research into the exact environmental and health benefits of each plant variety still needs to be done, many initial studies—undertaken by bodies as varied as NASA and a number of universities worldwide—have come to the conclusion that plants act as a kind of "pollutant sponge." This means they absorb all kinds of nasties in the atmosphere, from carbon dioxide to the various volatile organic compounds (VOCs) released from many common man-made products, including paint, carpets, furniture, and cleaning products. Plants are able to remove these toxins from the air through their leaves and stems, or through their roots via the potting soil, where small microbes turn the toxins into food for the plant. It's a win-win situation.

These VOCs are believed to be responsible for SBS (Sick Building Syndrome), that affliction of the modern-day office (see also page 137). Those affected can experience headaches; dizziness; fatigue; irritation of the skin, eyes, nose, and throat; and more serious ailments such as asthma.

Plants are good for your mental well-being, too; looking after and responding to something living is therapeutic. Again, work-focused studies have shown that having plants around can help reduce feelings of negativity, anxiety, depression, and stress. No one particular plant does this job better than any other, so to benefit from the positive psychological effects, choose a plant that you really like or feel connected to. That way, it will make you happy every time you look at it. Put simply, growing green things is good for your health as well as your home.

This page:
Plants, nature's oxygenators, will improve the air quality in your home. Groupings—such as this *Beaucarnea recurvata* (elephant's foot), *Philodendron scandens* (heart-leaf philodendron), and a selection of ferns—will have more impact health-wise than a single plant.

This page:
This display of easy-to-
care-for indoor plants
includes *Philodendron
scandens* (heart-leaf
philodendron), *Anigozanthos*
(kangaroo paw), various
cacti, *Sansevieria cylindrica*,
Aglaonema modestum
(Chinese evergreen),
Beaucarnea recurvata
(elephant's foot), some
Echeveria, and *Dracaena*.

CLEANING THE AIR

According to NASA, plants are nature's life-support system. The seminal Clean Air Study it undertook in the late 1980s found that the following plants were among the most effective at filtering toxins and pollutants from the air.

✳ *Aglaonema modestum* (Chinese evergreen). A lush-leaved, tough plant that can cope with drying out. Ideally it needs medium light but can cope with shade. Add some color by choosing a variety that has patterned foliage.

✳ *Anthurium scherzerianum* (flamingo flower). Another tough plant that can take a knock, tolerate a bit of neglect, and offer more or less continuous color. It needs medium light.

✳ *Chlorophytum comosum* (spider plant). As long as it gets a decent amount of light, this plant will pretty much look after itself.

✳ *Dracaena fragrans* 'Janet Craig' (corn plant). Really hardy, it can take low light and will tolerate drying out. It also stays compact.

✳ *Epipremnum aureum* (devil's ivy). Needs bright to medium light, and can tolerate drying out. A really great trailing plant.

✳ *Ficus benjamina* (weeping fig). Very good at processing toxins. Will thrive if well looked after. Give it a bright spot and leave it be, as it hates being moved—and don't let it dry out. Other members of the *Ficus* family, such as *F. lyrata* (fiddle-leaf fig) and *F. elastica* (rubber plant), are also good air filters.

✳ *Phalaenopsis* (moth orchid). Pretty, affordable, easily available, and about the toughest orchid out there. Give it a fairly bright spot and remember to soak the roots weekly or mist them daily.

✳ *Sansevieria trifasciata* (mother-in-law's tongue). As tough as old boots! Able to cope with dark corners and can be left to dry out between waterings. One of the few plants that gives off oxygen at night.

✳ *Spathiphyllum wallisii* (peace lily). A compact, hardy plant with lush leaves and a beautiful white flower. If it is left to dry out, it will usually recover with a good watering. Needs medium light. Sits well on a desk.

✳ *Zamioculcas zamiifolia* (ZZ plant). Particularly adaptable plant that tolerates both bright light and shade. Allow the soil to dry out between waterings.

HOUSEPLANTS & ALLERGIES

✳ According to the CDC (Centers for Disease Control and Prevention), 8 percent of people in the United States suffer from hay fever. The good news is that houseplants, which release few (if any) pollen spores, don't generally bring on bouts of hay fever. Unfortunately, if you are a sufferer, you are likely to have other allergies as well. In that case, avoid *Ficus* plants, particularly *F. benjamina* (weeping fig), which exudes a latexlike substance on its leaves that can trigger skin allergies.

✳ It's thought that growing houseplants can actually be a good thing for those with allergies, since plants act as natural detoxifiers and filters, removing pollutants and pollen spores from the air, and collecting dust particles on their leaves.

✳ Remember to clean your plants regularly to avoid any buildup of allergy-causing dust, and make sure you don't over-water, which can result in mold developing on the potting soil and plants, again leading to potential allergic reactions.

PLANT FAMILIES

BOLD

If you want to introduce just one plant into your home but also create the greatest impact with it, look to architectural plants. Among the tallest varieties of houseplants, and often featuring dramatic leaves, they are real talking points. Since they are so striking, they work well when displayed singly, as a focal point, rather than in a fussy group scheme. They should be positioned in such a way that their bold silhouettes are seen at their best—in an alcove or a corner that neatly frames them, or against a blank wall, for example. They lend themselves to the larger spaces in our homes, such as the living room, dining area, or even a generously sized bathroom or kitchen.

Lighting up the plant at night—similar to how a sculpture would be lit in a museum or gallery—is a pleasing touch. After all, such plants are, essentially, living sculptures, and if you think of them this way it will also help you decide where and how to display them. Bear this in mind when you look to buy one of these plants. Because of their size, they are investment pieces, so don't start your houseplanting career with one unless you feel confident that you will be able to care for it properly.

Among the plants that fall into this architectural category are tall foliage plants such as *Ficus benjamina* (weeping fig) and *F. benghalensis* (Indian banyan); sculptural-leaved varieties such as *Philodendron bipinnatifidum* (horsehead philodendron) and *Fatsia japonica* (Japanese aralia); palms, like *Dypsis lutescens* (butterfly palm), and false palms, such as *Dracaena fragrans* 'Massangeana' (corn plant); larger ferns like *Nephrolepis exaltata* (sword fern); and large-leaved climbers such as *Philodendron hastatum* (elephant's ear philodendron).

Above:
Euphorbia tirucalli (pencil tree) takes several years to reach this size. You would likely have to special order one this mature from a garden center.

Right:
One of the most popular indoor palms, *Howea forsteriana* (Kentia palm) is very handsome, as well as extremely low-maintenance.

TIP
....
False palms, so-called because their leaf growth resembles that of a palm tree, make attractive stand-alone feature plants. Included in this group of common larger houseplants is *Yucca elephantipes* (spineless yucca), *Beaucarnea recurvata* (elephant's foot), and *Pandanus baptistii* (screw pine).

FIVE STATEMENT PLANTS

* *Cycas revoluta* (Japanese sago palm). With its thick trunk and stiff fronds, this exotic-looking plant takes the same form as a palm tree, although it is not actually related to the palm family. Very slow-growing, with a leaf spread of 3 feet (1 m), it will eventually—after 50 to 100 years—reach a height of 20 feet (6 m). Position in bright but indirect light and away from radiators. Water frequently in the summer and sparingly in the winter.

* *Euphorbia tirucalli* (pencil tree). This attractive, unusual plant will grow up to 5 feet (1.5 m) tall, but have a spread of just 20 inches (50 cm), making it particularly suited to small or busy rooms. Its striking new growth has a pink tinge (which is why it's sometimes called "sticks of fire"). It needs very little care—just watering every two to three weeks in summer—but requires a lot of light.

* *Phoenix canariensis* (canary date palm). This classic-looking palm is very easy to grow, requiring just bright indirect light and moderate watering. It can grow up to 6½ feet (2 m) tall, with a spread of 5 feet (1.5 m).

* *Trachycarpus fortunei* (Chinese windmill palm). This decorative fan palm variety, so-called because of the shape of its leaves, has a wide spread (6½ to 8 feet/2–2.5 m), which makes it suited to larger spaces such as a living room or sunroom. It is slow-growing, highly adaptable, and flourishes in bright light. Water it regularly.

* *Yucca rostrata* (beaked yucca). This treelike yucca with bluish-tinged leaves looks great in a living room. It's easy to grow and maintain but needs bright light. Allow the top of the potting soil to dry out between waterings, and feed every two weeks during the growing season. This plant can become top-heavy, so you must rotate it regularly for even growth. It can grow up to 15 feet (4.5 m) tall and 3 feet (1 m) wide.

EDIBLE

If you're unable to grow crops outdoors, why not create a bit of a kitchen garden right inside your house? After all, there's nothing quite so rewarding as growing your own fresh food. As well as looking good, these crops in their containers also mean that you will always have a few essential cooking ingredients at hand.

The idea of growing your own food is for most people a rather romantic idea, but if you're planning to do so indoors, you must be realistic about what is actually possible. The edible plants that work best in a domestic setting are the smaller kinds, such as herbs, a dwarf citrus, baby salad leaves, or the smaller varieties of tomatoes, such as cherry or baby plum. Use established starter plants if you can, as they'll have a better chance to flourish than a plant started from seed.

Once you've succeeded with easier crops such as herbs, and if you like the idea of expanding your repertoire, why not try the likes of carrots, radishes, potatoes, and the dwarf varieties of beans? However, do bear in mind that all these plants will take up more room than the more obvious indoor edibles suggested on the right.

One other thing worth considering is that edible plants needn't be confined to the kitchen—as long as they receive plenty of bright light, they can also be welcome additions in other parts of the house, such as a dining room or sunroom.

TIP

Edible crops are best grown in glazed ceramic or plastic planters, with plenty of drainage at the bottom. They won't dry out as quickly as terracotta pots.

FIVE EASY INDOOR CROPS

* *Capsicum annuum* var. *annuum* Grossum Group (sweet/bell pepper). Enjoys bright, indirect sunlight and should be watered liberally in spring and summer but less in winter. Peppers look good planted in terracotta pots and grouped on shelves.

* *Capsicum annuum* (chili pepper). Grows as small, shrublike bushes, with fruits in a range of vivid greens, reds, yellows, and oranges. (A green chili is an unripe red one.) Highly decorative, they make satisfying indoor plants. They need a warm, bright window ledge and moist soil, but be careful not to over-water.

* Herbs need a bright, sunny spot, such as the windowsill. Keep the soil moist, but don't be tempted to over-water. *Allium schoenoprasum* (chives), *Coriandrum sativum* (coriander/cilantro), *Mentha* (mint), and *Ocimum basilicum* (basil) are all worth growing indoors, as are *Artemisia dracunculus* (tarragon), *Origanum majorana* (marjoram), *O. vulgare* (oregano), and *Salvia officinalis* (sage).

* Salad leaves come in all shapes and colors, from the classic *Lactuca sativa* (lettuce) to bitter *Cichorium endivia* (endive), and peppery *Eruca sativa* (arugula) to pretty *Valerianella locusta* (lamb's lettuce). Different varieties planted together look brilliant—try packets of mixed seeds—as well as juxtaposed with other more ornamental plants, such as *Zamioculcas zamiifolia* (ZZ plant) and *Aloe variegata* (partridge breast aloe). They need plenty of bright light, so a sunny window ledge is ideal. Keep them well watered.

* *Solanum lycopersicum* (tomato). Incredibly easy to grow in the right conditions, bearing abundant fruit in summer and into early fall. They require very similar care to *Capsicum* and should be grown in a warm, bright spot. Feed weekly with a tomato feed.

This page:
Herbs in individual
pots are easy to care for,
arrange, and harvest.
This selection includes
Mentha (mint), *Ocimum
basilicum* (basil), and
Coriandrum sativum
(coriander/cilantro).

This page:
Pots of *Lavandula* (lavender)
are a simple way to
introduce some soothing
scent and seasonal color
into your home.

FLOWERS & FRAGRANCE

Smell is probably the most evocative of our senses—the faintest whiff of something familiar can transport you back to a different time or place.

Introducing scented varieties into an arrangement of houseplants can also create an additional layer of interest. The same can be said of flowering plants. While the majority of plants that do well in our homes tend to be foliage varieties, there are some flowering plants that can also adapt to the growing conditions indoors. They are more delicate than the hardy or architectural houseplants, so if you plan to invest in some, you will also need to give them the love and attention they need.

Make sure you don't waste a plant's particular scent by clashing it with another perfumed variety. In the confines of a room, one type of perfumed plant is usually enough, and typically, more is more—think about how a mass of *Hyacinthus* (hyacinths) will have a much more pronounced perfume than a single bulb.

The various greens of foliage plants have a neutral hue that tends to fit easily into any room's decorating scheme. While it's not a deal-breaker, it's worth paying attention to the depth and shade of the color of any flowering plants you hope to introduce into a space, just to make sure it will fit in with the overall look.

TIP

Scent is not confined to flowering plants; many edible plants also give off a lovely fragrance—just think of herbs such as mint, basil, and lemon thyme.

FIVE FABULOUS FRAGRANT PLANTS

* *Citrus*. Easy-to-obtain citrus plants such as *Citrus* x *microcarpa* (calamondin orange) and the less common *Citrus* x *limon* (Tahitian orange) provide a wonderful Mediterranean scent in addition to small fruits. They're great in kitchens and dining areas, particularly when displayed alone. Place in a bright spot and rotate to ensure even growth. Allow it to dry between waterings, and keep it out of drafts.

* *Gardenia jasminoides* (gardenia). These plants are high-maintenance but worth the effort for their fragrance. The contrast between the dark green leaves and the white flowers is stunning. Ideal bathroom plants (they love humidity), position them near sunny windows, as they need bright, indirect light. Never let the soil dry out completely, but be careful not to over-water. Mist daily.

* *Jasminum* (jasmine). *Jasminum polyanthum* (pink jasmine), which is the most common variety as well as the easiest to grow indoors, is spring-flowering; white *J. officinale* (poet's jasmine) blooms from summer into fall. Position one by a bright window and keep the soil moist. Daily misting will help maintain the pretty blossoms. The climbing stems will need support.

* *Oncidium* orchids. The small, bright, (usually) yellow flowers make for a cheerful springtime display and look wonderful en masse in bathrooms and bedrooms. They prefer filtered light—think frosted glass. Allow them to dry out between waterings.

* *Stephanotis floribunda* (Madagascar jasmine). The glossy leaves and white, fragrant flowers work well in groups. They are ideal to fill a bedroom with scent. Water frequently in summer, sparingly in winter. Mist daily to prevent buds from dropping. The climbing stems will need support.

FIVE FANTASTIC FLOWERING PLANTS

* *Aechmea fasciata* (urn plant). Technically speaking, this is not a flowering plant. The striking, bright-pink "flower" is actually a set of leaves on a stalk growing out of the center of the lower rosette of leathery leaves. This "urn," designed to collect water, should have water in it all times, but it is important that these plants are never waterlogged. They prefer bright, indirect sunlight and are well suited to window ledges. Their bold, tropical appearance makes them a colorful addition to a planting scheme.

* *Medinilla magnifica* (rose grape). These dramatic plants bear rose-pink flowers that droop spectacularly, provided they are kept in as humid an atmosphere as possible—which makes them perfect for bathrooms. You will need to mist them constantly in spring and summer to encourage and maintain the flowers. They can grow to over 3 feet (1 m) in height and spread, so they tend to function best as stand-alone feature plants.

* *Streptocarpus* (Cape primrose). These are now one of the most popular flowering houseplants. Relatively easy to care for, they come in a variety of colors, with blue-purple being the most common, and they flower throughout the summer. They like bright, filtered, indirect light and need to be watered regularly. They're useful plants for adding a splash of color to a landscaped group.

* *Vanda* orchids. These unusual and versatile orchids come in a variety of colors, but the most striking is a rich, deep blue. Plants will live happily without potting soil as long as the roots are misted every day or submerged in water for an hour once a week. They have the most impact when displayed en masse, so hang them at different heights to create a living screen or curtain.

* *Vriesea splendens* (flaming sword). The dramatic flowers can grow well over 3 feet (1 m) tall, but with a narrow spread. Like *Aechmea fasciata* (see left), they are a bromeliad and so the leaves form a natural vase that needs to be kept topped off with water. As long as this "vase" is filled, you won't need to water the soil unless it dries out. These plants like bright, indirect sunlight and look great on their own because of their strikingly striped leaves and overall form.

TIP

Many of the prettiest flowering bulbs, such as *Muscari* (grape hyacinth) and *Convallaria majalis* (lily-of-the-valley), also emit a delicious perfume.

THE CASE FOR CUT FLOWERS?

We can all agree that a flower is a thing of beauty and that every space is brightened up with the addition of a bunch or two. But if you are weighing the benefits of regularly buying flowers against investing in a flowering houseplant—or two—consider this. Although the United States produces its own supply of cut flowers (California is the main source), many are imported from far locales, such as South America. Most houseplants sold in Europe are grown in big greenhouses in the Netherlands and, due to their longevity, are transported to their destinations overland. Mixed bouquets of cut flowers, on the other hand, have a shorter life span and may clock up a lot of air miles flying from their countries of origin. So not only do flowering houseplants give a display that lasts and lasts, they score points on the eco front as well.

This page:
Grouping together a
collection of the same
family of plants, such as
these *Phalaenopsis*, *Cattleya*,
and *Dendrobium* orchids,
is one of the easiest ways
to develop a display.

This page:
Slow-growing *Aglaonema modestum* (Chinese evergreen) can tolerate lower light levels than many houseplants, which makes it particularly versatile.

TOUGH & TOLERANT

These are the kinds of plants to choose if you have never grown houseplants before, or are nervous that you aren't especially green-thumbed. Happy to be neglected and best kept on the dry side, they are suitable in most locations in the home. These types are also highly adaptable, and many of them can survive in lower light levels. They usually stay pretty compact and work well when arranged in groups, either in repetition or mixed up with other plants.

If you're at all unsure about what to buy when shopping for tough and tolerant plants, look out particularly for succulents and cacti. There are now hundreds of varieties of both types of plant available, and they are all fairly indestructible. Using succulents as your guide for finding other tough-to-kill plants is a pretty good safeguard. Plants with similarly thick and fleshy foliage store water in their leaves like succulents do, and are likely to be somewhat self-sustaining as well—think along the lines of *Kalanchoe blossfeldiana* (flaming Katy) and *Ficus elastica* 'Decora' (rubber plant).

TIP
Getting water on the leaves of succulents or on cacti will damage them, so water by standing plants in a saucer full of water and letting them absorb what they need until the top layer of potting soil is moist.

TOP THREE SUCCULENTS

* *Crassula ovata* (jade plant). These exotic hardies require good light and little water. They have beautifully plump, glossy green leaves that are tinged with red, and they retain a bushlike appearance. They're fun, low-maintenance plants—ideal for children's bedrooms—and they look good as part of a shelfie arrangement.

* *Kalanchoe tomentosa* (panda plant). The green leaves are covered with small silver hairs, giving this plant a blue-gray appearance. It should be placed by a bright window. Be careful not to over-water, and do cut off dead flower stems and pinch back leggy growth to keep plants looking their best.

* *Sempervivum tectorum* (common houseleek). This succulent is sometimes called "hens and chicks" because it produces its own offspring—miniature "chick" plants offset from the mother "hen." There are many varieties available and all of them seem to thrive on neglect. They work well as part of a living wall design (see page 59).

SUCCULENT SURVIVAL TIPS
Though succulents are generally tough houseplants, they do make a few demands.

* Succulents prefer bright, natural light.

* They need to be watered generously during the summer months, when their fleshy leaves grow plumper with all the water stored in them.

* Allow them to dry out between waterings because they hate being waterlogged.

* Succulents are more tolerant of the cold than you might expect. This is because they originate from desert regions, where the temperatures can drop very low at night.

TOP FIVE TOLERANT PLANTS

✻ *Aglaonema* (Chinese evergreen). The 21 species of *Aglaonema* all have attractive oval-shape leaves growing from a stalk in a variety of leaf colors, many of them with pretty variegated white markings. All need moderate watering, and while the all-green varieties, such as *A. modestum*, don't mind lower light levels, the variegated ones, like the silvery-gray *A. 'Silver Queen,'* need brighter light, though not direct sunlight. They are slow-growing and look particularly good when grouped together.

✻ Cactus plants. These come in a wide variety of shapes and sizes, and many flower in the spring and summer. Most are desert plants and so require very little water and virtually no care. Most cacti enjoy bright sunlight and can be displayed in well-lit rooms and on window ledges. It's important to keep the soil well drained and not to over-water. They look great in clusters, grouped on shelves and tabletops. Some cacti can grow to several yards tall and look striking as single plants in heavy terracotta pots.

✻ *Dracaena fragrans* (corn plant). These plants need good light levels, but they should be kept out of direct sunlight. You only need to water them moderately, and even less in winter. Any pruning should be done in spring. They can reach 6½ feet (2 m) tall, but their spread is fairly compact, which makes them ideal for corners and tight spaces.

✻ *Epipremnum aureum* (devil's ivy). These plants require little care and only average light levels, so keep them out of direct sunlight. Their attractive leaves make them particularly striking in hanging and trailing schemes, such as along a shelf edge or in a hanging planter. Prune plants in spring to prevent them from becoming stringy over time.

✻ *Spathiphyllum wallisii* (peace lily). Of all the flowering houseplants, the peace lily is perhaps the easiest to care for. They prefer bright, indirect sunlight but can tolerate lower light levels. For the plants to bloom, however, they do require brighter light. The attractive white flowers appear in early summer and can last for weeks.

This page: This tabletop display of tough and tolerant plants includes *Ficus pumila* (creeping fig) in the gold bowl; a grouping of *Echeveria* in the zinc pot; and a mature *Beaucarnea recurvata* (elephant's foot) by the window.

TIP
....
Cacti are often thought of as being a separate group of plants, but all of them are, in fact, succulents.

THE INDESTRUCTIBLES

The following ten plants positively thrive on neglect and, provided that you put them near a natural light source and water them occasionally, they should fight off your best efforts to send them to that big greenhouse in the sky. Most can, in fact, go without water for up to a month. They can also deal with changes in temperature, as well as tolerate drafts.

TOP TEN (VIRTUALLY) INDESTRUCTIBLE PLANTS

✷ *Aloe.* While these succulents need bright light, they can be allowed to dry out between waterings. They also grow slowly, so you won't have to keep repotting them.

✷ *Aspidistra elatior* (cast-iron plant). These obliging plants can take a lot of abuse. They have tough leaves that don't mind drafts, changes in temperature, and darker locations. They also don't mind drying out between waterings.

✷ *Chlorophytum comosum* (spider plant). As long as you give spider plants reasonable levels of light, you can pretty much forget about them.

✷ *Echeveria.* As with aloes, these succulents require bright light, but they can be left to dry out between waterings. They are also slow growers, so there is no need to repot them.

✷ *Fatsia japonica* (Japanese aralia). These tough-leaved plants can withstand children and large pets brushing by them roughly, and can also deal with changes in temperature and drafts. They require a decent amount of light, and they don't mind drying out a little bit between waterings.

✷ *Ficus elastica* 'Decora' (rubber plant). This particular *Ficus* is much better at dealing with reduced light than its cousins. These plants can also be allowed to dry out between waterings.

✷ *Howea forsteriana* (Kentia palm). Here is another tough-leaved plant that doesn't mind being around children and large pets. It can also take reduced light levels.

✷ *Sansevieria trifasciata* (mother-in-law's tongue). These robust plants can take darker spots in the house, don't mind drying out between waterings, and also remain compact, which makes them ideal for hallways and foyers.

✷ *Tradescantia* (wandering Jew). These trailing plants can cope with neglect as long as they are in a reasonably light spot. They look good when allowed to grow wild but can also be pruned back quite a bit.

✷ *Zamioculcas zamiifolia* (ZZ plant). These compact plants are happy to dry out and can take a dark location.

CONTAINERS

POTENTIAL PLANTERS

If you put your mind to it, you can use pretty much anything as a container for an indoor plant. The containers you choose will depend on the look of your home and the overall effect you wish to achieve. Over-the-top, mix-and-match vintage pitchers, cups, and teapots can look just as striking as slick, modern, geometric containers—it's all about context. Take into account the shape, scale, and look of the actual plant you are potting, too—a *Howea forsteriana* (Kentia palm), for example, naturally lends itself to a complementary woven raffia basket, but it can look just as fabulous in a contrasting square metallic planter.

But before you go all out on the creative front, you need to check that your chosen container is large enough for the root ball of your plant and that it is waterproof. Also, be aware of the weight and size of the container.

Ian is very experimental when it comes to planters. He will attach air plants to old bottle corks or lightbulbs before hanging them in his foyer or kitchen, or create a miniature indoor garden in an old tin bathtub, sink, or vintage suitcase. He has been known to landscape his fire grate for the summer. Once you start looking at every vessel as a potential planter, you'll be surprised at how inventive you can be.

POTTING HOUSEPLANTS

* It's always best to plant directly into your chosen container, after taking the plant out of the plastic pot it came in.
* If your container isn't waterproof, add a liner by painting the inside with either waterproof sealant or pond liner paint. You can also opt instead for some thick, industrial plastic sheeting—again, think of the pond lining variety—to create a barrier.
* Add drainage, such as gravel, small stones, or broken-up terracotta pots, to the base of the container. Aim for a depth of about one-fifth the overall volume of the pot.
* Follow this with a layer of general-purpose potting soil. How thick this should be will depend on the size of the pot and the plant's root ball—for example, a small root ball in a tall pot will need to sit on a thick base of soil to get it to the right height.
* Position the plant(s) in the pot—in the center if there's only one—and slowly add more soil, firming it down as you go.
* Water the plant. If it's a plant that prefers dry conditions, don't go overboard.
* Add some surface dressing, if desired, such as a layer of moss to give the plants a professional finish and help them retain moisture (see right).

* Ideally, repot plants at the start of every spring, especially if you are only going up one pot size, i.e., to one that is slightly bigger than the root ball. Add some fresh potting soil and a little plant feed. If you have several plants in a pot and wish to thin them out, this is the time to do it.
* Keeping your plants in small containers can slow down growth. But to ensure they stay healthy, keep them in the same pot for a maximum of three to four years before repotting into a slightly larger container.

TIP
....
The bigger the container, the lighter the material it should be made from—think wicker or plastic. This is particularly relevant if the plant is going to be moved around fairly often.

MOSS TOPPINGS

* The two most common types of moss to use are flat moss, which is green, or reindeer moss, a type of lichen which is naturally white, but is also available in other colors.
* Mist the moss every time you water the plant. If it dries out, give it a good soaking and its color will come back.
* Don't forage moss yourself—buy it from garden centers or florists.
* Moss may attract unsightly sciarid flies (see page 168) if your plant is somewhere dark and damp.
* Instead of using moss as a surface dressing, try slate chippings, pebbles, gravel, or wood chips. They will help your plant retain moisture, although not as well as moss.

Left:
Containers for indoor planting schemes come in all shapes, sizes, and materials. Simply choose those that suit your particular style and will achieve the desired look.

CONTAINER MATERIALS

The beauty of container planting is that by trying out different shapes, materials, finishes, and colors, you can quickly alter the finished look of your arrangement. Do this over time and your plant design can evolve along with your changing tastes and general trends.

Your containers can make a massive difference to the overall mood of your display—a classic terracotta pot, for example, has a very different feel from a high-shine metal planter.

It's now easy to source containers in as many materials and finishes as you can name. Whether your preference is for earthy hewn woods, woven baskets, and aged terracotta or slick brass, copper, and marble-effect finishes, someone out there will have the container of your dreams.

When choosing containers, look at both the shape and the shades of your plant. Do you want the pot to disappear into the background, so the plant takes center stage, or do you want to use it to reflect the plant's shape or offset its colors?

Take a look at the area where you intend to place the pots. The two most effective approaches are to have pots that either complement the space and so blend in, or wildly contrast with it, thereby making a statement. For a group of plants, you'll need to decide if you want pots of the same material and size, or different sizes for each container, or perhaps different styles but united by the same finish. Each decision will make a difference to the final look.

TIP

Create a simple focal-point display by planting an attractive bowl with seasonally appropriate bulbs: Think *Narcissus* 'Tête-à-Tête,' which is a dwarf daffodil, in spring, and *Cyclamen persicum* (Persian cyclamen) at Christmas.

This page:
Crackle-glazed and
chalky terracotta pots of
Portulacaria afra 'Variegata'
(elephant food), *Echeveria
agavoides* 'Taurus' (molded
wax), and *Pteris cretica* var.
albolineata (white-striped
Cretan brake).

This page:
A small terrarium lends itself to an intimate planting scheme. From left: *Sedum adolfi* (stonecrop), *Crassula ovata* (jade plant), and an *Echeveria*, finished with *Cladonia rangiferina* (reindeer moss).

Originally a feature of over-furnished Victorian parlors, the terrarium is undergoing a serious revival. This is due in no small part to the fact that the glass vessel conveniently creates a microclimate, meaning it can be positioned pretty much anywhere as long as the plants inside get sufficient light and warmth.

Clever planting that plays on the relationship between the lines and shapes of the container and the plants inside make terrariums a strong design statement. The impact will be greater if you use either a single plant, such as *Echeveria elegans* (Mexican gem), or create a mini landscape with multiple plants of two or three varieties, such as *Asparagus setaceus* (asparagus fern) with a *Nertera granadensis* (bead plant) or some small cacti. Species of *Tillandsia* (air plant) are a great choice for a minimalist-style terrarium because they take their water and nutrition from the air.

RETURN OF THE TERRARIUM

Above left:
A fishbowl works surprisingly well as a simple terrarium. Add interest with different shapes of succulents and cacti.

Below:
An open terrarium allows for attractive plant overspill, such as trailing plants draped over the edge or plants growing out of the top, like this cactus.

TOP TERRARIUM PLANTS

* *Aloe*
* *Begonia rex* (King Begonia)
* *Chlorophytum comosum* (spider plant)
* *Crassula ovata* (jade plant)
* Ferns (smaller forms; see page 134)
* *Hedera* (ivy)
* *Hypoestes phyllostachya* (polka dot plant)
* *Peperomia caperata* (emerald ripple)
* *Dionaea muscipula* (Venus fly trap)
* *Tillandsia* (air plant)

Note: Air plants, ivies, and ferns will all do especially well in closed terrariums.

This page:
This arrangement of geometric terrariums is planted with *Asparagus setaceus* (asparagus fern), a selection of succulents, *Sansevieria trifasciata* 'Golden Hahnii' (mother-in-law's tongue), and *Asplenium nidus* (bird's nest fern).

TERRARIUMS

✳ For closed terrariums, choose plants that prefer low to medium light levels and moist potting soil.

✳ Open terrariums are like low-maintenance mini gardens, where the plants need higher light levels and more frequent watering.

✳ Drainage is key in open terrariums. Before adding the potting soil, line the bottom with a layer of gravel from ½ to 1 inch (1–3 cm) thick, depending on the size of the terrarium.

✳ Choose plants with small leaves, slow rates of growth, and a high tolerance for humidity.

✳ Experiment with your design ideas outside the terrarium first; it's much easier to make changes when you have a bit of space.

✳ You can buy miniature long-handled tools for planting and maintaining a terrarium, but an improvised tool kit comprising a fork and spoon, long-handled tweezers, and a chopstick or two can be just as effective.

✳ Finish your arrangement with an attractive layer of moss, gravel, or small pieces of bark.

✳ Once everything is in place, use a clean, dry cloth to gently wipe the inside of the glass.

Groups of terrariums work really well, so experiment with using them in the same design but in different sizes, or have a collection with a similar theme, such as three or four vintage apothecary bottles. Mix and match your vessels, from fishbowls to mason jars, hurricane lamps to glass. Just remember to choose glass-sided containers that will comfortably enclose the plants to help create that essential microclimate, restrict any drafts, and allow you to see what is growing inside. As to where to put terrariums, they work really well on desks and dining tables, or as decorative features in their own right on a display shelf or a high-standing lamp table.

Terrariums need virtually little or no maintenance, depending on whether they are open or closed. Closed terrariums create their own water cycle, meaning they basically look after themselves. Any maintenance issues are more about keeping the glass nice and clean to show off the plants at their best.

TIP

Zeoponic is a newly developed form of water-retaining gravel that Ian likes to use for both terrarium and normal container planting. Keep an eye open for it—it will be coming to a garden center near you soon.

This page:
Using a small terrarium as a container can turn a single plant, such as this *Sansevieria trifasciata* 'Golden Hahnii' (mother-in-law's tongue), into a statement piece.

DESIGNING
WITH PLANTS

WHERE TO START

When deciding on a plant scheme, it works well if you are able to treat your plants as part of the overall room design, rather than as an add-on. That said, however, many of us decorate our homes piecemeal, room by room, meaning that the elements that bring real personality to a space tend to come some time after the hours spent poring over paint charts and choosing furniture.

First, take a good look at the space where you want the plants to go, to get a sense of its overall feel and arrangement. What have been your design influences? What style of furniture do you have? What kind of art is on display? What is your main color scheme? Accent colors? Where, exactly, are you hoping to put the plants?

Next, collect images of plants you are drawn to, as well as containers and stands you like, plus planting ideas that appeal—Pinterest is a useful tool for this. Light is incredibly important for a plant's survival so, before you buy, research whether your proposed location will meet the lighting requirements of your selected plants. You also have to decide on the care, commitment, and time you are willing to give. There is absolutely no point in coming up with, say, a striking "indoor jungle" scheme if, realistically, you are not the kind of person who is going to regularly dust down, prune, and correctly water the plants.

You really don't need to have masses of plants to make a statement—it all comes down to how they are arranged and displayed. And remember that the space between your plants is as important as the plants themselves. Choosing plants of the same color or perhaps using the same container in different sizes will create a cohesive design.

Another point to consider is whether you have a view of a garden or other green landscape. A really successful design scheme can involve bringing that exterior inside by planting around the window to frame the view. (Conversely, if you are facing a brick wall, you can conceal the view.) This has the effect of both extending and reflecting the outside world. Adding a few elements that you would normally expect to find outdoors, such as weathered terracotta pots or exterior planters, is another neat way of linking indoors and out.

In terms of current design trends, it's all about the group. The days of a solitary stand-alone plant have gone—unless, of course, we mean a beautiful indoor tree or a huge feature plant that can act as a living sculpture. Grouping is a really simple styling trick, but its impact can be huge. We prefer to group our plants or containers in odd numbers—three, five, seven, and so on.

TIP

If you're in any doubt about a design approach, keep your ideas clean, simple, and tidy.

Above:
Create a breathtaking still life by placing indoor plants in complementary containers and combining them with striking objects, such as these three *Aloe* *variegata* (partridge breast aloe), an *Asparagus setaceus* (asparagus fern), a *Spathiphyllum wallisii* (peace lily), and an *Asplenium nidus* (bird's nest fern).

Other key design styles we think are also really worth a try are terrariums (everyone loves a self-contained, self-sufficient indoor garden); hanging plants with the aid of macramé and sky planters; and landscaping shelves, mantelpieces, or windowsills with a considered grouping of plants and other *objets*.

PLANT LANDSCAPING

If you are grouping plants together to create a landscape effect, it's good to work with contrasts. Go for opposites: tall uprights, such as a *Ficus*, with low-growing bushy plants like *Tradescantia zebrina* (silver inch plant); or a small-leaved plant, such as a *Peperomia caperata* (emerald ripple), next to one with broader leaves, perhaps a *Spathiphyllum wallisii* (peace lily). Alternatively, choose plants with different shades of foliage and add in a few feature flowering plants that pick up on the leaf colors.

Wooden beads—reminiscent of
nature, travels, and texture

A living wall at L'Atelier
de Joël Robuchon,
Covent Garden, London

Sunflowers in bloom

Eames Black Wire Chair by
Swiss design company Vitra

Architectural splendor—
Monstera deliciosa

A Mini in Havana, Cuba

Princess of Wales Conservatory,
Kew Gardens, London

St Pancras Building,
Kings Cross, London

A white house beneath
a blue sky in Cyprus

Paul Smith—an inspirational
fashion and design hero

The Yves Saint Laurent Garden,
Marrakech, Morocco

Peraliya Buddha Statue,
Tsunami Memorial, Sri Lanka

Orange Panton by Vitra

The Living Workstation at the
RHS Chelsea Flower Show 2011

Palms at the Movie Colony,
Palm Springs, California

Stained glass
at the Ivy Restaurant,
Covent Garden, London

An herb table

Kinder Aggugini catwalk,
London Fashion Week 2011,
Fall/Winter

SCALE & CONTRAST

Scale is a brilliant device to play around with, and if you use it well, you don't need an enormous amount of space in which to be creative with your planting. Emphasizing the contrast between little and large, such as pairing two different plants with similar foliage but of totally different sizes—for example, a *Howea forsteriana* (Kentia palm) with a *Washingtonia robusta* (Mexican fan palm) or a *Sansevieria trifasciata* with a *S. cylindrica*—is a simple but effective design trick.

For a group scheme that packs a punch, be creative with your containers or plant choices. Groups offer endless possibilities for developing an arrangement. They can also form a focal point in a room that previously had none, or help set the decorative tone.

There are several different ways to achieve such a scheme. Just think about the infinite varieties of container shapes, sizes, colors, and materials available. Add to that the range of plants you might pick and you'll see how much fun you can have creating a mix-and-match arrangement.

Containers can create very different design themes, from vintage chic to slick minimalism. To give a collection coherence, aim for a little consistency in some part of it, whether in the materials of the containers, their shape, or the plants themselves—a single variety or plants from the same family, for example. Another option is to choose a color theme for your pots: think pastels or primaries, neons or monochromes.

Look outside for plant inspiration. Public gardens and parks are all about medleys, with various plants of different shapes, colors, and sizes bringing out the best in each other. Such an approach can be translated into a striking houseplant arrangement.

Below:
Put plants together with similar foliage shades, like this *Aeonium arboreum* 'Atropurpureum' (houseleek tree) and *Begonia rex* (King Begonia), for a coherent look.

Right:
Pair a tall plant, such as *Ficus cyathistipula* (African fig tree), with a squat one, like *Aglaonema* 'Silver Queen' (Chinese evergreen). Similar leaf shapes and containers give unity.

TOP TEN STAND-ALONE PLANTS
* *Beaucarnea recurvata* (elephant's foot)
* *Dracaena fragrans* (corn plant)
* *Fatsia japonica* (Japanese aralia)
* *Ficus benjamina* (weeping fig)
* *Ficus lyrata* (fiddle-leaf fig)
* *Howea forsteriana* (Kentia palm)
* *Monstera deliciosa* (Swiss cheese plant)
* *Philodendron scandens* (heart-leaf philodendron)
* *Schefflera* (umbrella tree)
* *Yucca elephantipes* (spineless yucca)

SYMMETRY & REPETITION

Below left:
Placing a pair of matching plants, such as these *Anigozanthos* (kangaroo paw), at either end of a mantelpiece, shelf, or table is a simple design trick that will surely please the eye.

Below right:
A mix of *Echeveria elegans* (Mexican gem), *Crassula ovata* 'Gollum' (Gollum jade plant), *C. ovata*, and *Portulacaria afra* 'Variegata' (elephant food) is consistent with containers of a similar finish.

52

If you don't feel confident enough about experimenting with different looks, there are two simple tricks of the trade you can use that will always result in a successful display: symmetry and repetition. These straightforward but effective devices are pretty much foolproof. Think about a pair of matching *Spathiphyllum wallisii* (peace lily) at either end of a mantelpiece, or the same single plant, such as *Zamioculcas zamiifolia* (ZZ plant), in identical planters lined up on the treads of a staircase.

The reason symmetry and repetition work so well is because they please the eye: A symmetrical display looks tidy, while one plant used over and over again creates impact. A lone *Phalaenopsis* (moth orchid) can appear insignificant, whereas a pair looks deliberate and four makes a statement.

Similarly, small plants such as *Aloe vera* (Barbados aloe) can sometimes disappear into the background of a room, but massed together they will command attention.

Using repetition, whether of the plant variety or the planting method, creates a feeling of abundance and generosity in a decorative scheme. A large planter filled with several of the same variety of *Carex morrowii* 'Variegata' (Japanese grass sedge) or *Nephrolepis exaltata* 'Bostoniensis' (Boston fern), for example, makes for a fabulous centerpiece. Plants placed symmetrically on shelves or across the tops of cabinets can have the effect of giving a sharp, finished look to a room. Making patterns of symmetry or repetition—or even both—the foundation of your first display is a great option for a novice plantsperson.

This page:
Alternating planters of
two different styles is a
simple design device for
displaying a collection
of plants from the same
family, in this case ferns.

This page:
Put a spare surface to good use
by displaying a an assortment of
plants interspersed with artwork.
From left: *Epipremnum aureum* (devil's
ivy), *Asplenium nidus* (bird's nest
fern), an *Echeveria*, *Nephrolepis exaltata*
'Bostoniensis' (Boston fern),
Philodendron scandens (heart–leaf
philodendron), *Asparagus densiflorus*
'Myersii' (plume asparagus),
Peperomia rotundifolia, *Ficus elastica*
(rubber plant), and another
Philodendron scandens (heart–leaf
philodendron).

This page:
Wall-hung box shelves are a neat way to frame and protect smaller plants like *Kalanchoe sexangularis* (paddle plant), *Senecio rowleyanus* (string of pearls), *Sempervivum tectorum* (common houseleek), and *Crassula perforata* (string of buttons).

ALTERNATIVE DISPLAYS

There are as many different ways to display your houseplants as there are plants you can use. On the following pages, we look at some of our favorites, but there's no doubt that if you put your mind to it, you will come up with some original ideas of your own. Just keep in mind the size, shape, and color of your container and where you want to position it in the room. Then you can think of inventive ways to make the different elements work together.

Above left:
Bushy *Chlorophytum comosum* (spider plant) and ferns are given a sharper finish when displayed in a minimalist plant stand.

Above right:
Vintage hampers are used to display *Philodendron scandens* (heart-leaf philodendron), a variety of ferns, and *Rhipsalis paradoxa* (chain cactus).

Single-plant shelves

Tiny, individual shelves—with just enough room for one pot—or decorative wall sconces are really attractive ways to present plants, especially in an awkward space. You can arrange a series of floating shelves on a wall, adding to them over time as you build up your plant collection. For the affordable DIY version, get a lumber yard to cut the wood to size for you. Otherwise, seek out companies that specialize in home accessories (see pages 169–170).

Box shelves

Box shelves are a variation of the floating shelf. They effectively frame the item that's placed inside—in this case, a plant in a pot—transforming

Above:
Make the most of a dramatic trailer, such as this *Rhipsalis paradoxa* (chain cactus), by investing in a stand that suits the growth style of a particular plant.

Right:
A collection of ferns teamed with a *Rhipsalis baccifera* (mistletoe cactus) is shown off to perfection in a glass display cabinet.

Hanging planters

At the mention of hanging plants, most people instantly hark back to the macramé planters that were so in favor during the hippy heyday of the 1970s. Now they are very much back in vogue among the hipster contingent.

Modern macramé planters can look fantastic when styled well. Try grouping them together or hanging them in a line, perhaps at slightly different heights. Or play off their feel against a slick, minimalist interior. Take a look at the work of British jewelry designer Eleanor Bolton (see page 169), who has created a collection of knotted rope planters in a range of both monochrome and contemporary accent colors that will effectively style your plants for you.

Hanging planters aren't just made out of macramé, however; you can now find them in a variety of styles and materials, from cute glass baubles for air plants to modernist ceramic pieces. Then there are the larger-scale, flat hanging trays that allow you to display a group of plants together—IKEA does a good affordable version.

Though hanging planters are a wonderful way of displaying plants at a different viewpoint, they're not just suited to homes that have high ceilings—a low-hanging plant positioned in the corner of a room is particularly arresting because it is so unexpected.

Wall planters

Essentially pots attached directly to the wall, these planters are the perfect solution if you don't have many available flat horizontal surfaces for displaying your plants. They work well in spaces where there is a lot of passing traffic, such as the kitchen, entryway, or bathroom, because they are securely held in place out of the way. As with floating or box shelves, they suit awkward or dead spaces, too—try positioning them in a vertical line up a tall wall, in the gap next to a door or a window frame, above a nightstand, and so on.

it into a statement display. Box shelves work particularly well in children's rooms because the box helps protect the plants from any accidental knocks. Used singly, these shelves create impact, but you can also add to them over time without reducing their appeal.

Box shelves are easy to come by in good interiors stores or on the internet. Don't forget to double-check dimensions to make sure they are large enough to accommodate your chosen plant and its container.

Peg boards

Remember those holey boards of plywood your dad used for hanging his tools from hooks in the garden shed or garage? Well, it's time to reclaim them for your plants. Spray-painted or varnished, then accessorized with a selection of wall planters attached with "S" hooks, they make an adaptable display area that is both portable and interchangeable.

Living walls

These are essentially vertical gardens. A few years back, when living walls first came into vogue, their proponents used them for elaborate facades to cover the outsides of buildings or to disguise ugly walls in a garden. Now the whole idea has been shrunk down to a domestic scale and you can buy ingenious wall-hanging planters that enable you to create your own indoor living wall.

You could, of course, be very ambitious and plant an entire wall from floor to ceiling, but a more manageable approach is to view your living wall as you would a large mirror or painting, and invest in a wall planter of an appropriate size and scale. Make sure you attach it securely to the wall, then simply plant it up. Trailing plants such as *Epipremnum aureum* (devil's ivy), *Tradescantia* (wandering Jew), and *Rhipsalis baccifera* (mistletoe cactus) suit this approach especially well.

Plant stands

Forget their granny associations—plant stands are a neat and efficient way to give a floor-standing plant an extra design dimension. They are also a useful device for introducing height to a floor-based scheme. Whether it's the retro wire-frame look that interests you or the slicker feel of an integrated planter and stand, there is a design out there for you. Alternatively, you can, of course, play around with placing a large pot on a small stepstool to create a similar effect.

RIGHT PLANT, RIGHT ROOM

LIVING SPACES

For most of us, the living room is the showcase of our homes, where we express our personal style. It is often the room that people choose first when deciding where to make their decorative mark on a property. As well as being a personal place of relaxation, it is also the main public-facing room in our homes, the space where we welcome in other people.

Houseplants can have an enormous impact here because living rooms, by the nature of their layout and usual design, offer plenty of areas and opportunities for creative plant arrangements. Just think of the surfaces and parts of the living room that can make welcome homes to a houseplant: mantelpieces, windowsills, shelves, corners, side tables—the permutations are as endless as your imagination.

If you spend a lot of time in your living room, and you've always hankered after a plant that's a real showstopper, this is probably the place to put it. A mature *Ficus benjamina* (weeping fig), *Philodendron bipinnatifidum* (horsehead philodendron), *Dracaena marginata* (Madagascar dragon tree), *Beaucarnea recurvata* (elephant's foot), or *Euphorbia tirucalli* (pencil tree) are all great conversation pieces.

And if your living room is spacious enough, you could go to town with creative combos by clustering together different-size, floor-based architectural palms into a focal point, or by dotting an arrangement of individually potted succulents along the mantelpiece instead of the typical collection of unremarkable knickknacks.

Even better, choose plants in foliage colors that complement and enhance your favorite ornaments to create a living still life. The stems of trailing plants such as *Hedera helix* 'Sagittifolia' (English ivy) or *Rhipsalis paradoxa* (chain cactus) look dramatic draped over the edge of shelves and high cabinets, while a terrarium is a bold, self-contained feature that's perfect for a coffee or side table.

A good houseplant really can complete the look of your living room, provided you consider the aesthetic impact of your indoor garden on the overall space and are also conscious of the practical growing requirements—in terms of light and heat—of the plants you are picking.

FIVE OF THE BEST TRAILING PLANTS
* *Epipremnum aureum* (devil's ivy)
* *Hedera helix* (English ivy)
* *Mikania scandens* (climbing hemp vine)
* *Rhipsalis baccifera* (mistletoe cactus)
* *Tradescantia* (wandering Jew)

This page:
A low side table makes a
useful display surface
in a living room for a
cluster of *Beaucarnea
recurvata* (elephant's
foot), *Philodendron scandens*
(heart-leaf philodendron),
Rhipsalis baccifera (mistletoe
cactus), and a variety
of ferns.

LARGE-SCALE DISPLAYS

Above:
A Victorian hothouse-style room with *Dracaena marginata* (Madagascar dragon tree), a succulent terrarium, *Ficus microcarpa* 'Ginseng' (Indian laurel), *Ficus benjamina* (weeping fig), *Euphorbia tirucalli* (pencil tree), *Asparagus densiflorus* 'Myersii' (plume asparagus), *Ficus elastica* 'Decora' (rubber plant), *Howea forsteriana* (Kentia palm), *Philodendron xanadu*, and *Portulacaria afra* 'Variegata' (elephant food).

Right:
Groups of odd numbers are pleasing to the eye and are a simple but effective design tool to use with plants. From left: *Howea forsteriana* (Kentia palm), *Washingtonia* x *filibusta* (Washington palm), *Howea forsteriana* (Kentia palm), and *Trachycarpus fortunei* (Chinese windmill palm).

The living room is usually the biggest room in the home, which is why it tends to lend itself to more grand displays. A large-scale display is one that is tall or bold, or involves a sizable group of several different plants and containers.

This type of setup can serve several purposes: to create a focal point in a room that previously didn't have one; to separate and screen off different areas within the room; to disguise unsightly views; or simply to act as a beautiful piece of living sculpture.

FIVE STATEMENT FLOWERING PLANTS
These bold beauties will bring a sense of drama to any setting.
* *Anthurium scherzerianum* (flamingo flower)
* *Medinilla magnifica* (rose grape)
* *Spathiphyllum wallisii* (peace lily)
* *Tillandsia cyanea* (pink quill)
* *Vanda* orchids

Above:
A mix of *Rhipsalis baccifera* (mistletoe cactus), *Epipremnum aureum* (devil's ivy), *Philodendron scandens* (heart-leaf philodendron), and *Asplenium nidus* (bird's nest fern) makes a voluminous shelfie above the single pots scattered below.

Above right:
Plants from the same family create a coherent display. This lineup includes *Chamaedorea elegans* (parlor palm), *Rhapis excelsa* (lady palm), and *Washingtonia x filibusta* (Washington palm), with a floor-standing *Howea forsteriana* (Kentia palm).

Be aware that a tall, architectural, floor-standing plant, such as a *Monstera deliciosa* (Swiss cheese plant) or a *Carnegiea gigantea* (saguaro), can be quite expensive to buy because it will have taken the grower several years to get it to maturity. Having said that, these are also the plants that really make a statement in themselves, so you do in fact get a lot of bang for your buck in terms of making an impact.

However, if cost is a consideration, another way to create height (if that's the way you want to go in a large-scale display) is to use your pieces of furniture to give medium- or smaller-size plants

a bit of a leg up. Try grouping them together on a side table or stool, or use a plant stand to achieve the same effect. Otherwise, invest in some tall, open shelves, which you can put to use as a room divider, and fill them with row upon row of individually potted plants—a straightforward idea that looks really striking.

Or how about turning the height idea on its head and look to the ceiling, instead of the floor, as your starting point? There are a plethora of different styles of hanging planters now available, in materials as varied as macramé, metal, and marble. Attach them to hooks in the ceiling to create an arrangement at eye level. This is also a great technique for using plants as a screening device, either by repeating the same type of plant in a line or by hanging the plants at different heights. Orchid curtains work really well for this, too. They look spectacular and are surprisingly simple to achieve with *Vanda* orchids, which behave a bit like air plants and can be simply hung from hooks at varying heights.

Left:
For such a small plant, a *Tillandsia* (air plant) makes a big statement and, because it lives on air, it can be dotted in and around other objects. The examples here slot in neatly with a delicate display of animal bones.

Right:
Draw attention to diminutive plants such as this *Echeveria* and smaller varieties like this *Asplenium nidus* (bird's nest fern) by using decorative containers or dynamic angular framing devices.

INTIMATE DISPLAYS

69

Intimate displays are all about creating close-up interest. They are not concerned with the wham-bam effect of a striking, large-scale arrangement, but are more about attention to detail.

Consider the color, texture, and design of your containers—at this level they are often as significant as the plants—as well as the outline form, foliage tones, and leaf shapes of the plants you want to use. Think of the difference in look between an *Opuntia microdasys* (bunny ears cactus), an *Aloe variegata* (partridge breast aloe), and a *Nephrolepis exaltata* (sword fern) to see what we mean.

Intimate displays can bring life to forgotten corners: the edge of a mantelpiece, a narrow spot on a windowsill, the top of a piano. They are also a useful device for drawing the eye to interesting, unusual, or quirky details within a room.

Even though the dimensions you are working with are considerably smaller than those of a large-scale display, you can still put to use some of the same design techniques. For example, try grouping plants of different heights and

appearances, such as a small upright *Ficus elastica* (rubber plant), a bushy *Asparagus setaceus* (asparagus fern), and a draping *Philodendron scandens* (heart-leaf philodendron), or combining complementary shades, like a *Begonia rex* (King Begonia) and an *Aeonium tabuliforme* (flat-topped aeonium).

Consider as well the style, material, and color of the furniture on which the arrangement is displayed. A group of tall cacti will give a vintage rosewood cabinet, for example, a moody look; a couple of bold *Hippeastrum* (amaryllis) will add impact; while a bowl of scented *Hyacinthus* (hyacinth) will lighten it up entirely.

A little container garden can make a darling intimate display, but remember that it will be easier to look after if you use the same type of plant or choose varieties with similar light and watering needs. Then there is the current design favorite, the terrarium, which now comes in a large range of shapes and materials, and can evoke a unique sentimentality deserving of a double take.

MANTELS & FIREPLACES

Below left:
Even a narrow mantel can be used as a display surface, provided you choose small varieties of plants, such as *Tillandsia* (air plant).

Below right:
The texture of this basket complements the plants growing inside: *Howea forsteriana* (Kentia palm), *Washingtonia x filibusta* (Washington palm), and *Rhapis excelsa* (lady palm).

70

Even if a fireplace isn't used for its original purpose, in most living rooms it will still be the main focal point. It is also really easy to style up with plants. If it is still in use, choose heat-tolerant plants such as succulents, cacti, and *Tillandsia* (air plant), and avoid trailing plants.

Individual plants in separate pots allow you to rearrange at will, while a trough of complementary plants creates a simple, stylish statement. Symmetrical mantel displays can work well, as can repetitive designs. For another look, divide the space into vignettes, introducing plants alongside ornaments. A mantel can also take one bold plant, such as an *Anthurium scherzerianum* (flamingo flower), *Zantedeschia aethiopica* (calla lily), *Dendrobium* orchid, or *Medinilla magnifica* (rose grape).

For the hearth, group both tall and squat plants, such as *Zamioculcas zamiifolia* (ZZ plant), *Calathea makoyana* (peacock plant), and *Epipremnum aureum* (devil's ivy). For the grate, try *Zamioculcas zamiifolia* as the backbone, *Rhipsalis baccifera* (mistletoe cactus) for trailing, and *Aglaonema* 'Silver Queen' (Chinese evergreen) for foliage color accents.

RECIPE: EASY-CARE MANTEL DISPLAY
2 *Begonia rex* (King Begonia)
1 *Beaucarnea recurvata* (elephant's foot)
1 *Peperomia caperata* (emerald ripple)
2 *Echeveria setosa* (Mexican firecracker)

This page:
Houseplants can be interspersed with favorite ornaments for a more personal display. From left: *Aloe vera*, an *Echeveria*, *Portulacaria afra* 'Variegata' (elephant food), and *Zamioculcas zamiifolia* (ZZ plant) on the mantel, and *Platycerium bifurcatum* (staghorn fern) decorating the hearth.

This page:
One plant per pot keeps rearranging easy: *Aeonium arboreum* 'Atropurpureum,' (houseleek tree), *Begonia rex* (King Begonia), *Beaucarnea recurvata* (elephant's foot), *Begonia rex* again, *Portulacaria afra* 'Variegata' (elephant food), *Echeveria agavoides* 'Taurus' (molded wax), and *Pteris cretica* var. *albolineata* (white-striped Cretan brake).

OTHER DISPLAY IDEAS

Put side and lamp tables to good use by enlisting them as supporting surfaces for eclectic clusters of mix-and-match plants, positioning taller plants at the center or back of the display, with smaller ones around the edges or front.

Draw the eye upward by using the tops of cabinets and high shelves as plant zones. This approach works particularly well in rooms with high ceilings, or if the furniture in question has interesting detailing. Plants on a high shelf can draw attention to architectural details nearby, such as cornicing and coving, picture rails, panels, or plasterwork.

Plants can populate shelves in a variety of ways, acting as spacers between collections of books or as a means of highlighting some of your favorite decorative items. You can also make a line of matching plants the sole occupant and, therefore, the key feature of one shelf, or employ trailing and draping plants—think *Aporocactus flagelliformis* (rat's tail cactus), *Hedera helix* 'Eva' (English ivy), or *Ficus sagitatta* 'Variegata'—as a means of softening up the rigid, hard lines of a shelving system. The possibilities are endless.

Don't feel, though, that you must confine your plants to the obvious living room locations. Put your mind to how you can use unexpected display areas for your plants. Engage other pieces of furniture to be a part of your scheme. A couple of plants on a serving cart, for example, can really bring it to life—and it works even better if the plants are herbs that can perk up your cocktails. You can also use spare chairs, tray tables, small step ladders, and piles of magazines as surfaces on which to place your pots.

How and where you display your plants is all about being a bit relaxed in your approach. After all, if you don't like an idea or think it doesn't work, you can always shift them to another spot.

Top left:
Saving space with *Euphorbia tirucalli* (pencil tree) and *Portulacaria afra* 'Variegata' (elephant food), *Pteris cretica* var. *albolineata* (white-striped Cretan brake).

Bottom left:
A serving cart is a unique display for *Washingtonia* x *filibusta* (Washington palm) and *Asparagus densiflorus* 'Myersii' (plume asparagus).

Top right:
Use spare chairs and side tables to display plants, such as these succulents, including *Aloe variegata* (partridge breast aloe) and *Echeveria agavoides* 'Taurus.'

Bottom right:
This stepstool is transformed into a plant stand with a large *Ficus carica* (common fig) on the top step, and a small *Peperomia rotundifolia* on the bottom.

RECIPES: THE PERFECT SHELFIE

2 *Sansevieria trifasciata* (mother-in-law's tongue)
2 *Zamioculcas zamiifolia* (ZZ plant)
3 *Epipremnum aureum* (devil's ivy)
3 *Beaucarnea recurvata* (elephant's foot)

OR

3 *Rhipsalis paradoxa* (chain cactus)
3 *Sansevieria trifasciata* (mother-in-law's tongue)
2 *Beaucarnea recurvata* (elephant's foot)
2 *Maranta leuconeura* (prayer plant)

SEASONAL FLOWERS

Bulbs and flowering potted plants bring additional color and variety to indoor displays. Most spring bulbs suit being planted en masse in a large container, but they also grow well and look rather good in a hanging planter. The larger flowering bulbs, such as *Hippeastrum* (amaryllis) and *Zantedeschia aethiopica* (calla lily), are usually so bold and dramatic that you don't need to do much to make them look good—just place them in a position that shows off their sculptural lines.

Above:
Bring outdoor plants, such as *Hydrangea macrophylla* (common hydrangea) indoors for a short period for some seasonal color.

TIP
....
As a general rule, flowering plants need more light than foliage varieties. Bear this in mind when deciding where to display them. Position them in a bright spot and turn the pots regularly.

FLOWERING PLANTS BY SEASON

SPRING
Clivia miniata (Natal lily), *Crocus chrysanthus* (Golden crocus), *Hyacinthus* (hyacinth), *Narcissus cyclamineus* 'Tête-à-Tête' (daffodil), *Primula vulgaris* (primrose)

SUMMER
Argyranthemum frutescens (marguerite), *Centaurea cyanus* (cornflower), *Lavandula* (lavender), *Paeonia* (peony), *Rosa* (rose), *Rosmarinus officinalis* (rosemary)

FALL
Calluna vulgaris (heather), *Chrysanthemum morifolium* (garden mum), *Physalis alkekengi* (Chinese lantern), *Solanum capsicastrum* (winter cherry)

WINTER
Cyclamen persicum (Persian cyclamen), *Euphorbia pulcherrima* (poinsettia), *Hedera helix* (English ivy), *Hippeastrum* (amaryllis), *Ilex* (holly), *Jasminum nudiflorum* (winter jasmine), *Schlumbergera truncata* (Christmas cactus)

IDEAS FOR CHRISTMAS

* Line up miniature *Araucaria heterophylla* (Norfolk Island pine) and *Cyclamen persicum* (Persian cyclamen) dressed with moss. Or swap the trees for diminutive *Hedera helix* (English ivy), *Ilex* (holly), and *Rosa* (rose).
* Display bowls of *Hippeastrum* (amaryllis) underplanted with *Ilex* (holly) and *Hedera helix* (English ivy) on tables and ledges.
* Individual pots of *Hippeastrum* work brilliantly placed up a staircase.
* *Euphorbia pulcherrima* (poinsettia) looks wonderful when displayed en masse.
* Group three Christmas trees, such as *Picea abies* (Norway spruce), of varied heights and decorate each one differently. Try wiring miniature terracotta pots of tiny *Cyclamen persicum* (Persian cyclamen) or *Rosa* (rose) onto the branches.

This page:
A group of miniature
Rosa (rose) in
complementary pots
makes a pretty tabletop
display in summer. Put
the plants back in the
garden when they have
finished flowering.

12

PLANTS FOR LIVING SPACES

Aechmea fasciata
Common name:
Urn plant
Light: Bright light
Care: Lightly water
the plant's roots, and
replenish water in its
reservoir when it dries out.
Tips: Epsom salts and
bright light can be used
to induce a pinkish-
orange bloom in spring.

Araucaria heterophylla
Common name:
Norfolk Island pine
Light: Bright
indirect light
Care: Keep the soil moist.
Tips: Turn the plant
regularly to promote even
growth, and trim only the
lower branches.

Ficus lyrata
Common name:
Fiddle-leaf fig
Light: Bright to
moderate indirect light
Care: Keep the soil moist.
Tips: Clean and polish
the leaves regularly, and
prune the top leaves to
promote bushiness.

Ficus microcarpa 'Ginseng'
Common name:
Indian laurel
Light: Bright
indirect light
Care: Keep the plant
moist, and mist regularly.
Tips: Prune regularly to
retain the plant's shape;
for every six to eight leaves
that grow, prune two back.

Begonia rex
Common name:
King Begonia
Light: Bright
indirect light
Care: Water the plant
lightly, and keep the
soil moist.
Tips: Nip off buds and
blossoms to help maintain
large, healthy leaves.

Clivia miniata
Common name:
Natal lily
Light: Moderate light
Care: Keep the soil
slightly moist.
Tips: Keep the plant in
cool temperatures to
encourage flowering
in early spring.

Schefflera elegantissima
Common name:
False aralia
Light: Moderate to bright
indirect light
Care: Drench the plant
and then allow the
surface soil to dry
before rewatering.
Tips: Repot the plant
annually in spring,
but don't put it in too
large of a pot.

Echeveria elegans
Common name:
Mexican gem
Light: Bright light
Care: Keep the soil
slightly moist.
Tips: Remove the
offshoots and propagate
them to prevent the
pot from becoming
overcrowded.

Medinilla magnifica
Common name:
Rose grape
Light: Bright
filtered light
Care: This plant enjoys
high humidity and
moderate watering.
Tips: Prune the plant
back to half its size after
flowering to promote
future blossoms.

Phalaenopsis
Common name:
Moth orchid
Light: Moderate to
bright indirect light
Care: This plant enjoys
high humidity.
Tips: Cut the stem back
to the second notch from
the base after flowering to
encourage future blooms.

Streptocarpus hybrids
Common name:
Cape primrose
Light: Moderate to
bright light
Care: Keep the soil moist.
Tips: Pot this plant
in small containers to
prevent root rot. Pinch off
old flowers to encourage
new growth.

Tillandsia cyanea
Common name:
Pink quill
Light: Bright light
Care: Mist the plant
twice weekly to keep
the soil moist.
Tips: Keep the plant
cool in winter to
encourage spring blooms.

KITCHENS & EATING SPACES

It's said that the kitchen is the heart of the home, so why not show yours a little love with some creative living decor? Just remember, before you start on any design scheme, it's always helpful to think about which plants might work the best in a particular space.

Though it might be something of a cliché, herbs are the obvious choice for a kitchen. They work on a practical level because they are an invaluable cooking ingredient, while their fragrance can also mask any unpleasant odors. Aesthetically, they can also create a really attractive feature—try placing a large container of mixed herbs on the table as part of a decorative setting, or plant individual varieties of herbs in separate matching containers and line them up along a shelf, a windowsill, or, space permitting, a work surface.

One thing you should be aware of is that herbs do need a little care and attention. They like good light, and the different varieties can have quite particular watering requirements. Other edible plants such as the different *Citrus* species or *Capsicum annuum* (chili pepper) are also attractive additions to the kitchen.

There is something about that vibrant chlorophyll green of healthy, thriving, growing plants that just belongs in a kitchen—perhaps

Above:
Indulge your sense of fun with the containers you choose. This llama-shape pot makes a playful and original planter for a *Peperomia rotundifolia*.

Right:
Ferns, including this *Nephrolepis exaltata* 'Bostoniensis' (Boston fern), will thrive in the humid conditions found in a kitchen.

because it is often the room that links to any outdoor space there may be. To make the most of that inside-outside flow, look for plants that can tolerate the heat and humidity found in a kitchen—think *Asplenium* ferns and the various *Echeveria* succulents. *Chlorophytum comosum* (spider plant), and, perhaps surprisingly, *Phalaenopsis* (moth orchid) also enjoy the environs of a kitchen. As long as you find a bright spot for them, they will thrive.

Left:
Create your own indoor kitchen garden with a selection of edible plants, such as *Citrus japonica* (kumquat), *Citrus x microcarpa* (calamondin orange), mixed herbs, and *Capsicum annuum* (chili pepper).

Below:
A selection of plants at different heights—from left, *Aglaonema modestum* (Chinese evergreen), *Ficus lyrata* (fiddle-leaf fig), *Begonia rex*, and *Philodendron xanadu*—adds interest to a formal dining space.

FIVE VERY USEFUL INDOOR HERBS

The following herbs all prefer a light, bright position, such as a sunny windowsill. Ideally, check them every couple of days to see if they need watering because they really hate drying out. Misting them occasionally doesn't hurt, but make sure you don't over-water. Avoid buying supermarket herbs if at all possible—they are grown and treated in such a way as to last for only a short time. Instead, buy your plants from a garden center.

* *Allium schoenoprasum* (chives)
* *Coriandrum sativum* (coriander/cilantro)
* *Mentha* (mint)
* *Ocimum basilicum* (basil)
* *Petroselinum crispum* (parsley)

TABLETOPS

Having something attractive to look at every day while going about our chores in the kitchen can lift the spirits to no end. And it doesn't have to be an elaborate affair to produce the desired effect. Our absolutely favorite idea is to have one fairly substantial planter filled with a group of the same plants. A basket filled with a mix of *Asplenium* ferns with different foliage colors and leaf shapes looks fabulous, while a rush basket of grasslike *Carex morrowii* 'Variegata' (Japanese grass sedge) will gently sway in any breeze. Just make sure the container you choose is of a size that you can easily lift and carry in case you need to clear the decks; in a kitchen space, portable is practical.

Positioning your chosen display off-center—at one corner or to one end of the kitchen table—is an effective look. The stems of a trailing *Rhipsalis paradoxa* (chain cactus) or two draped over a corner or an edge is unexpected but striking. Likewise, try a collection of plants you wouldn't necessarily associate with a kitchen, such as the delicate-looking *Phalaenopsis* (moth orchid), which comes in a whole kaleidoscope of colors.

If the table is wide enough, put the space in the middle to good use with a neat, orderly row of plants. Be conscious of the scale of the plants you choose, though. There is nothing more annoying than not being able to see people seated around the table because of an arrangement that is either too tall or too broad.

Above and below:
Grouping together the same plants or plants of the same family in one large container makes for an impressive tabletop display. A rush basket complements the group of *Beaucarnea recurvata* (elephant's foot) planted inside (above), while a selection of ferns lightens the look of a recycled rubber basket (below).

FIVE SUCCESSFUL KITCHEN PLANTS

* *Asparagus setaceus* (asparagus fern)
* *Chlorophytum comosum* (spider plant)
* *Ficus microcarpa* 'Ginseng' (Indian laurel)
* *Phalaenopsis* (moth orchid)
* *Soleirolia soleirolii* (mind-your-own-business)

This page:
The gentle look of a
Phalaenopsis (moth orchid)
is an unexpected choice
for a kitchen, but it makes
a striking tabletop display
here, teamed with *Pteris
cretica* var. *albolineata*
(white-striped Cretan
brake) and *Nephrolepis
exaltata* 'Bostoniensis'
(Boston fern), all in
white containers.

Left:
Create a natural flow between house and garden by placing plants by a door, such as this *Dracaena fragrans* (corn plant), which has the advantage of growing slowly and staying narrow.

Right:
Ficus lyrata (fiddle-leaf fig), one of the most eye-catching houseplants, thrives in a position near a glass door or window, on the threshold between inside and out.

BRINGING THE OUTSIDE IN

Most indoor plants are evergreen, so having them in your home means that even in the depths of winter you will get a hit of nature to boost your mood. And when the great outdoors is thriving and growing, houseplants emphasize the link between inside and out. So play up your room with a view and turn your kitchen into a bit of a garden room. Add a single plant—or an assortment—to those areas that connect the outdoors with indoors, namely windows and doors, to create a natural flow between the two.

Tuck one light-loving, floor-standing, architectural plant such as *Ficus lyrata* (fiddle-leaf fig) or *Dracaena marginata* (Madagascar dragon tree) into a corner by the kitchen door. If you have the space, be adventurous and create a sort of free-form, modern sunroom feel with a jungle of mixed plants. Think hanging containers and floor-standing planters, and perhaps introduce another surface—some low steps, a plant stand or a barstool, for example—to support plants of a medium scale. Allow your group to spill into the room a little for a relaxed feel.

Windows lend themselves to simple repetitive plant compositions. If the sill is wide enough, you have a ready-made plant zone. If it's not, think laterally. Hanging planters are a useful tool. You could also put up a narrow shelf across the window and add some little pots and plants: succulents such as *Echeveria elegans* (Mexican gem) and trailers like *Hedera helix* (English ivy). Alternatively, buy a little herb planter (a pot with a coordinating drip tray), a narrow trough, or an indoor window box and position it directly in front of the window. *Asparagus setaceus* (asparagus fern), *Ficus benjamina* (weeping fig), and *Chlorophytum comosum* (spider plant), in particular, favor this kind of position.

FIVE THRIVING THRESHOLD PLANTS

✳ *Araucaria heterophylla* (Norfolk Island pine)
✳ *Ficus lyrata* (fiddle-leaf fig)
✳ *Hedera helix* (English ivy)
✳ *Philodendron xanadu*
✳ *Tetrastigma voinierianum* (chestnut vine)

TIP

Avoid positioning plants, and herbs in particular, close to the stove because of fluctuations in temperature.

WORK SURFACES

Practical plants are probably your best bet for a kitchen work surface. Place herbs or other edibles within easy reach of the chef's prepping area and keep decorative plants out of the way.

Filling a garden basket with a selection of different herbs keeps them contained as well as looking good, while a cluster of individual pots of herbs is practical and pretty—even better if you plant them in vintage terracotta pots. Recycled tin cans with striking graphics—think Italian tomatoes or Greek olive oil—also lend themselves

to a kitchen garden. Place the containers on a large decorative tray or chopping board to hold the arrangement together.

Try to keep your work surface display organized and compact so it doesn't take up too much room. A neat sequence of the same style of container sums up this look, but it doesn't mean you can't be a little imaginative with it. Look at the materials you have used elsewhere in the kitchen—the work surfaces, tile, cabinets, appliances, and so on—and work with them when choosing your containers.

If your work space is really limited, remember that just one plant can have impact in a room if it is placed in the right position. Look to the ends of your countertops or the corners of an island unit and use those spots for one beautiful, bold, commanding plant.

Above left:
Containers with clean lines suit modern kitchens. From left: *Chlorophytum comosum* (spider plant), *Mentha* (mint), and *Ocimum basilicum* (basil).

Above right:
A garden basket filled with a selection of herbs is the logical choice for a plant on a kitchen counter.

COMPACT COUNTERTOP PLANTS
* *Aloe vera* (Barbados aloe)
* *Echeveria elegans* (Mexican gem)
* *Mentha* species (mint)
* *Parodia chrysacanthion*
* *Zamioculcas zamiifolia* (ZZ plant)

This page:
A lineup of compact little cacti makes a delightful but unexpected display by the kitchen sink.

This page:
Use color-coordinated
containers to bring
coherence to a shelving
display of varied plants
and pots. Clockwise,
from top left: *Tradescantia*
(wandering Jew), *Aloe vera*
(Barbados aloe), *Peperomia
rotundifolia*, a selection
of succulents in the
terrarium, and *Maranta
leuconeura* var. *erythroneura*
(herringbone plant).

SHELVES

Positioning display plants on kitchen shelves at different heights adds interest and can give the impression of a very generous arrangement—even with a limited number of plants. Intersperse a set of shelves with plants of different shapes and sizes. Think of it as a vertical garden—for example, have trailing plants dangling from the top shelves, place taller plants lower down to draw the eye up, and balance it all out with bushy plants in the middle.

For high ceilings, make the most of the dead space above eye level and position a shelf about 12 to 20 inches (30–50 cm) below the ceiling. Fill it with pots of trailing plants, such as *Philodendron scandens* (heart-leaf philodendron) or *Epipremnum aureum* (devil's ivy), so they drape down the wall.

Most kitchen-friendly plants are green, but you can use your planters to pick up any accent colors or features you have in the room.

Above:
Shelves of small terracotta pots are an appealing choice and make a link between the kitchen and vegetable garden.

Below:
Create a vertical garden by positioning plants at different heights on a shelf system.

TOP PLANTS FOR SHELF DISPLAYS
BUSHY
* *Asparagus setaceus* (asparagus fern)
* *Asplenium nidus* (bird's nest fern)
TRAILING
* *Epipremnum aureum* (devil's ivy)
* *Philodendron scandens* (heart-leaf philodendron)
* *Rhipsalis paradoxa* (chain cactus)

Left:
This orchid collection, including *Cattleya*, *Dendrobium*, and *Zygopetalum*, suits this sunny position under a kitchen skylight because they are plants that like light and humidity.

Below left:
Quirky pots add personality to a small-scale display of *Hypoestes phyllostachya* (polka dot plant) and *Hedera helix* (English ivy).

OTHER IDEAS

If you think you're stuck with only obvious places for plants in your kitchen, slowly and carefully scan the whole room, from floor to ceiling, to see if you can find any little niches or unexpected spots to house a plant or two. The tops of cabinets, for example, lend themselves to plant displays, while a freestanding fridge would look all the better with some greenery featured on top.

Take advantage of any skylights and position light-loving plants, such as *Ficus benjamina* (weeping fig) or *Crassula ovata* (jade plant), underneath them—you may need to add a narrow wall shelf in order to do this. Alternatively, attach a piece of decorative trellis to a wall and hang planters from it.

Recycled vintage kitchen equipment, such as casseroles and colanders, teapots and tankards, make for charming details. If you want to expand on this idea, choose containers that either complement, match, or pick up on any feature colors in the dishwear you use.

If the kitchen is the family hub of the home, introduce some humor with planters in quirky shapes or designs: Think animals, vegetables, retro prints, and so on.

This page:
Build a tablescape by grouping together individually potted *Philodendron scandens* (heart-leaf philodendron) and *Epipremnum aureum* (devil's ivy).

12
PLANTS FOR KITCHENS & EATING SPACES

Anthurium 'Anthcandol'
Common name:
Flamingo flower
Light: Moderate to bright indirect light
Care: Water the plant thoroughly and do not allow the soil to dry out between watering.
Tips: Repot annually in spring, and keep the leaves clean and polished.

Crassula ovata
Common name:
Jade plant
Light: Bright light
Care: This plant tolerates high humidity, but keep the soil well drained.
Tips: Plenty of light and fertilizer improves the leaf color.

Phalaenopsis 'Rio Grande'
Common name:
Moth orchid
Light: Moderate to bright indirect light
Care: This plant can tolerate high humidity.
Tips: Cut the stem back to the second notch from the base after flowering to encourage future blooms.

Saintpaulia ionantha
Common name:
African violet
Light: Moderate to bright indirect light
Care: Allow the soil around the roots to dry out between waterings.
Tips: These plants bloom and bloom; pinch off old flowers to make way for future buds.

Dendrobium speciosum
Common name:
Rock lily
Light: Moderate to bright indirect light
Care: This plant can tolerate high humidity.
Tips: Plenty of fertilizer and regular watering promotes flowering.

Echeveria secunda var. *glauca*
Common name:
Glaucous echeveria
Light: Bright light
Care: This plant needs well-drained soil and can tolerate medium humidity.
Tips: Pinch off the blooms to preserve the appearance of the rosettes.

Kalanchoe blossfeldiana
Common name:
Flaming Katy
Light: Moderate to bright indirect light
Care: Water the plant only when the soil is dry.
Tips: Pinch off blooms after the flowers fade to preserve the look of the plant.

Nephrolepis exaltata
'Bostoniensis'
Common name:
Boston fern
Light: Moderate to bright indirect light
Care: Keep the soil moist.
Tips: Mist daily, and trim off any broken or brown fronds.

Schlumbergera truncata
Common name:
Christmas cactus
Light: Indirect light
Care: This plant tolerates high humidity. Keep the soil well drained.
Tips: To prevent flowers from dropping, avoid over-watering, under-watering, and other forms of stress.

Epipremnum aureum
Common name:
Devil's ivy
Light: Moderate to bright light
Care: This plant enjoys high humidity. Keep the soil moist, but do not over-water.
Tips: Prune twice a year to keep the plant looking bushy and full.

Spathiphyllum wallisii
Common name:
Peace lily
Light: Moderate to bright light; tolerates shade
Care: This plant thrives in high humidity. Keep the soil moist.
Tips: Remove flowering stems when the blooms turn green, and keep the leaves clean and polished.

Stephanotis floribunda
Common name:
Madagascar jasmine
Light: Bright light
Care: This plant tolerates high humidity, but keep the soil well drained.
Tips: Keep the plant cool in winter and ensure high humidity from spring to fall to promote flowering.

SLEEPING SPACES

Our bedrooms are our sanctuaries—the most private spaces in our homes to which we retreat in order to recharge our batteries. However, few adults today get the optimum eight hours' sleep to function at their best, and unfortunately, insomnia is on the rise. It seems we have lost the habit of good sleeping practices.

Creating a space where you can relax properly is a crucial part of developing what the experts call "good sleep hygiene," and plants can have an important part to play in this. Not only do they look good, they also help us to feel calm, and act as natural "air conditioners," gently raising humidity levels and improving air quality.

Look for plants that can cope with the slightly cooler temperatures and potentially lower light levels of the bedroom, and try to seek out the varieties that are proven toxin filters, such as *Philodendron scandens* (heart-leaf philodendron) and *Spathiphyllum wallisii* (peace lily). By happy coincidence, most of these plants are extremely attractive, with gently draping growth habits or softly swaying leaves, which means they slot neatly into a bedroom with a laid-back look.

You can take this approach to the next level by seeking out some of the few plants that act as nighttime oxygenators—in other words, those plants that improve air quality while you sleep.

TOP NIGHTTIME OXYGENATORS

Unlike most plants, the following behave counterintuitively, releasing oxygen at night instead of during the day. This is believed to be beneficial in a bedroom because it helps improve the quality of the air we breathe while we're sleeping. The bonus is that these houseplants are all very striking and will simply look good wherever they are placed.

* *Aloe vera* (Barbados aloe)
* Bromeliads such as *Aechmea fasciata* (urn plant), *Guzmania lingulata* (scarlet star plant), and *Tillandsia cyanea* (pink quill)
* *Dendrobium* orchids
* *Gerbera jamesonii* (Barberton daisy)
* *Hatiora gaertneri* (Easter cactus)
* *Phalaenopsis* (moth orchid)
* *Sansevieria trifasciata* (mother-in-law's tongue)
* *Schlumbergera truncata* (Christmas cactus)
* *Spathiphyllum wallisii* (peace lily)

TIP

Lavender oil is a traditional sleeping aid, but rather than shelling out cash on fancy lavender pillow sprays and lavender-filled eye masks—lovely as they are—why not introduce a lavender plant into your bedroom instead?

This page:
A procession of hanging planters is an imaginative way of displaying plants in a bedroom, shown here with *Rhipsalis baccifera* (mistletoe cactus), *Tradescantia* (wandering Jew), and *Epipremnum aureum* (devil's ivy).

This page:
A row of tiny trailing
Hedera helix (English ivy),
hanging down from
pots grouped on the
headboard, turns
what was a rather plain
bedside shelf into a
striking design statement.

NIGHTSTANDS

Whether your nightstand is a beautiful piece of furniture or a stack of vintage suitcases, it is essentially a practical space for keeping useful paraphernalia at hand, such as reading material, a table lamp, and an alarm clock. Given that there isn't much surface area to play with—and we are not in favor of style over substance or usefulness—any plant placed on a nightstand has the simple role of upgrading its look, particularly if it's in a lovely pot, and it has to be neat and compact.

If, however, there really is no space for a plant, no matter how small, you could attach a narrow ledge or shelf behind the table for a line of teeny individually potted plants such as miniature *Hedera helix* 'Sagittifolia' (English ivy) or *Aloe vera* (Barbados aloe). Placing a plant on the nightstand in a guest bedroom is a welcoming gesture.

Below:
The compact growth of *Sansevieria bacularis* 'Mikado' makes it perfect for sitting on this chair nightstand where there is little space to spare.

Below right:
A tray-based hanging planter is a novel way to showcase a selection of plants, like this collection of ferns and a *Maranta leuconeura* var. *erythroneura* (herringbone plant).

NEAT PLANTS FOR NIGHTSTANDS

- *Aeonium tabuliforme* (flat-topped aeonium)
- *Asplenium nidus* (bird's nest fern)
- *Dendrobium* orchids
- *Kalanchoe blossfeldiana* (flaming Katy)
- *Lavandula* (lavender)

This page:
Cattleya and *Phalaenopsis* orchids are nighttime oxygenators, improving the quality of the air we breathe as we sleep, which makes them a healthy choice for a nightstand.

BEDROOM HANGING PLANTS
BUSHY
* *Maranta leuconeura* (prayer plant)
* *Nephrolepis exaltata* 'Bostoniensis' (Boston fern)

TRAILING
* *Epipremnum aureum* (devil's ivy)
* *Hedera helix* (English ivy)

BUSHY & TRAILING
* *Chlorophytum comosum* (spider plant)

The top of a wardrobe or tall dresser is ideal for displaying plants. More often than not, this is a dead space and some plant landscaping will have lots of impact. It is also safely out of the way, so it's the perfect place for plants that are not particularly child- or pet-friendly.

The space on top of a dresser actually gives you lots of scope for experimenting with your plant styling—from a single statement flower to a simple row of the same type of plants, to a small mixed group to a full-on indoor border of bushy, medium-size, and trailing plants.

And looking up isn't just about the tops of furniture. Run laterally with the idea and you could find yourself adding an indoor tree. Because it is unexpected, the effect will be arresting. A *Dracaena fragrans* 'Janet Craig' or *D. fragrans* 'Massangeana' (corn plant) are always a good choice for their narrow spread and toxin-filtering properties. Other treelike plants that would work well are *Yucca elephantipes* (spineless yucca) and *Ficus cyathistipula* (African fig tree).

A single macramé pot holder hanging from the ceiling can also be surprisingly effective, as can a simple group or lineup of three individual planters hung at slightly different heights. Otherwise, opt for one large planter that can hold two or more plants; think of it as an indoor hanging basket.

LOOKING UP

Left:
Displaying a trailing *Scindapsus pictus* (silver vine), an assortment of ferns, and *Rhipsalis paradoxa* (chain cactus) in the dead space on top of a closet creates a lovely indoor border.

Above:
A vintage suitcase, set out of harm's way on a wardrobe, makes an innovative container for a selection of ferns and a *Rhipsalis paradoxa* (chain cactus).

WARDROBE BORDER PLANTS
* *Aglaonema* 'Silver Queen' (Chinese evergreen)
* *Asparagus setaceus* (asparagus fern)
* *Philodendron scandens* (heart-leaf philodendron)
* *Platycerium bifurcatum* (staghorn fern)
* *Rhipsalis paradoxa* (chain cactus)

OTHER SURFACES

Above:
Using the same type of pot lends coherence to different plants, here cactus, *Asplenium nidus* (bird's nest fern), and *Tradescantia cerinthoides* 'Variegata' (flowering inch plant).

Below:
Beaucarnea recurvata (elephant's foot) and *Guzmania* in their sparkly containers introduce color and interest to a practical dressing room.

Whether the style of your bedroom is boutique hotel chic, industrial luxe, midcentury retro, pared-back minimalist, or modern country, there will be a plant—and a container—to suit it.

As with other rooms in the house, you can view all surfaces and furniture as planting opportunities, from windowsills and mantelpieces to dressers and vanities. Landscape your chosen surface with a mix of decorative items and plants for a coordinated still-life effect. Less is often more with these types of displays, and a carefully chosen plant that fits in with the *objets* and look of the space can have real impact—like a *Scindapsus pictus* (silver vine) or pink-tinged *Tradescantia zebrina* (silver inch plant) trailing down the side of a dresser. Flowering plants can be used to introduce a jolt of unexpected color to the room: A single, bold, architectural *Guzmania lingulata* (scarlet star plant) or *Hippeastrum* (amaryllis) standing to attention is particularly striking.

You can also try neatly tucking a terrarium on the side of a vanity or dresser, or planting a larger vessel with a grouping of the same varieties, perhaps even positioned on the floor. If you happen to have a set of shelves, create a mini vertical garden, leading the eye from bottom to top with various plants speckled in between books, picture frames, and ornaments.

CLEAN-AIR STATEMENT PLANTS
* *Beaucarnea recurvata* (elephant's foot)
* *Chamaedorea seifrizii* (bamboo palm)
* *Chlorophytum comosum* (spider plant)
* *Dracaena fragrans* 'Janet Craig' (corn plant)
* *Dypsis lutescens* (butterfly palm)
* *Epipremnum aureum* (devil's ivy)
* *Ficus benjamina* (weeping fig)
* *Hedera helix* (English ivy)
* *Nephrolepis exaltata* 'Bostoniensis' (Boston fern)
* *Schefflera actinophylla* (Queensland umbrella plant)

This page:
The subtly pink tips of
a *Tradescantia cerinthoides*
'Variegata' (flowering
inch plant) give a gentle
lift to the neutral tones
used in this bedroom.

12
PLANTS FOR SLEEPING SPACES

Stephanotis floribunda
Common name:
Madagascar jasmine
Light: Moderate to bright indirect light
Care: Keep the plant moist or in high humidity, and reduce watering during winter.
Tips: Keep the plant cool in winter and ensure high humidity from spring to promote flowering.

Aloe vera
Common name:
Barbados aloe
Light: Bright light
Care: Keep the soil moist.
Tips: Avoid fluctuations in temperature.

Phalaenopsis
Common name:
Moth orchid
Light: Moderate to bright indirect light
Care: This plant tolerates high humidity, but allow the surface of the soil to dry out between waterings.
Tips: Cut the stem back to the second notch from the base after flowering to encourage future blooms.

Platycerium bifurcatum
Common name:
Staghorn fern
Light: Low to medium light
Care: This plant requires moderate moisture.
Tips: Mist the plant daily.

Chlorophytum comosum
Common name:
Spider plant
Light: Moderate to bright light
Care: Keep the soil moist.
Tips: An easy plant to grow and propagate—snip off the "babies" and replant them in a separate pot.

Gardenia jasminoides
Common name:
Gardenia
Light: Bright indirect light
Care: This plant tolerates high humidity; keep the soil moist but do not over-water.
Tips: This plant is beautifully scented but can be sensitive and doesn't always reflower.

Gerbera jamesonii
Common name:
Barberton daisy
Light: Moderate to bright light
Care: Keep the soil moist while in bloom but let it dry out slightly afterward.
Tips: Remove dead flowers to encourage blooming for as long as possible.

Hedera helix
Common name:
English ivy
Light: Bright light
Care: Allow the surface of the soil to dry between waterings.
Tips: This plant is a great trailing plant that can be trained into different shapes; keep it well pruned.

Sansevieria trifasciata
Common name:
Mother-in-law's tongue
Light: Moderate to bright light
Care: This plant doesn't require much water.
Tips: It's one of the easiest houseplants to look after! Keep the leaves clean.

Epipremnum aureum
Common name:
Devil's ivy
Light: Moderate to bright light
Care: This plant enjoys high humidity. Keep the soil moist, but do not over-water.
Tips: Prune twice a year to keep the plant looking bushy and full.

Spathiphyllum wallisii
Common name:
Peace lily
Light: Moderate to bright light; tolerates shade
Care: This plant thrives in high humidity. Keep the soil moist.
Tips: Remove flowering stems when the blooms turn green, and keep the leaves clean and polished.

Syngonium podophyllum
Common name:
Arrowhead vine
Light: Moderate light
Care: Keep the soil slightly moist.
Tips: Wear gloves when pruning, as this plant's sap can be irritating to sensitive skin.

BATHING SPACES

We have to walk a bit of a tightrope when designing and decorating our bathrooms. While their main purpose is to be practical, they are also havens, where we undertake the soothing rituals of cleansing and beautifying ourselves.

Most bathrooms tend to fall into one of two camps: light and humid or dark and humid. While light levels are obviously a key consideration when choosing plants for any space, with a bathroom you need to select humidity-loving plants above all. This means that cacti and most succulents are an absolute no-no. Instead, aim your sights at plants like orchids, ferns, and palms, which all like humidity and can also tolerate fluctuations in temperature.

Aloes are commonly associated with bathrooms—perhaps because they are a natural antiseptic—while the *Saintpaulia* (African violet)

is more than happy with the typically damp and humid conditions; conveniently, there is a rather cute micro-miniature variety, which is perfect for a small spot.

Ferns had their heyday during the Victorian era, but they are now having a bit of a style resurgence. As well as being perfect bathroom plants, because they thrive in damp conditions with low light levels, they also look pretty dramatic, too. Try a bold *Asplenium nidus* (bird's nest fern), a showy *Nephrolepis exaltata* 'Fluffy Ruffles' (sword fern), or an impressive *Platycerium bifurcatum* (staghorn fern).

When there is the space, bathrooms can lend themselves to some pretty spectacular plant displays: A pair of tall *Howea forsteriana* (Kentia palm) bookending a claw-foot bathtub look glorious, as does a living curtain of *Vanda* orchids draping down in front of a window.

How you use your bathroom will help you decide where to position the plants. A good starting point is to have plants within your sight line when taking a long, relaxing soak in the tub or an invigorating power shower. Even if your bathroom is spatially challenged, there is always

TIP

....

For a bathroom that's on the dark side, foliage plants are a better choice than flowering plants, which generally need more light.

HUMIDITY-LOVING PLANTS

* Ferns, such as *Nephrolepis exaltata* 'Bostoniensis' (Boston fern) and *Asparagus setaceus* (asparagus fern)
* *Guzmania lingulata* (scarlet star plant)
* *Saintpaulia* (African violet)
* *Spathiphyllum wallisii* (peace lily)

This page:
A spacious bathroom allows for an interesting variety of humidity-loving plants. From left: *Tradescantia* (wandering Jew), *Hedera helix* (English ivy), *Nephrolepis exaltata* (sword fern), *Schefflera* (umbrella tree), and *Peperomia scandens* 'Variegata' (variegated Cupid peperomia).

DR. ALOE VERA

The sap from *Aloe vera* (Barbados aloe) is brilliant at treating a number of skin ailments, including sunburn, eczema, and insect bites. If you grow one of these living pharmacies, here's how you should use the sap (but remember that it is most potent when used fresh):

* For treating just a small wound, break off a little, unobtrusive leaf or a small part of a leaf and gently rub the broken end onto the affected area.

* If the problem is larger, break off a whole leaf and let the sap drip from the bottom into a small container. Once it's finished dripping, rub the sap onto the wound with your fingers.

* If you need more sap, carefully cut the leaf open to extract any that's left inside.

room to introduce plants: Just choose miniature varieties and dot them in among your lotions and potions, or select plants that are slow-growing or happy with a robust pruning come spring.

Occasionally, the layout of a home has the bathroom slotted into an internal, windowless space. If this is the case with yours, you will just have to forget about using any plants here; no plant, no matter how resilient it is, can survive without access to natural light.

Above:
Aglaonema 'Silver Queen' (Chinese evergreen) makes an ideal bathroom plant, thriving in the moist air and tolerating shade.

Right:
A mature *Ficus lyrata* (fiddle-leaf fig) is a dramatic enough plant to make a strong statement all by itself.

Left:
A row of variously sized *Aloe variegata* (partridge breast aloe) in a single planter along the sink adds an invigorating burst of green to otherwise sterile bathrooms.

Below left:
Beaucarnea recurvata (elephant's foot), *Zamioculcas zamiifolia* (ZZ plant), *Asparagus setaceus* (asparagus fern), *Ficus microcarpa* 'Ginseng' (Indian laurel), and *Didymochlaena truncatula* (Mahogany Fern).

Just one well-chosen plant will create impact in a bathroom—think of a tall, narrow *Howea forsteriana* (Kentia palm) tucked into a corner, an effusive *Nephrolepis exaltata* 'Bostoniensis' (Boston fern) hanging down over one end of the bathtub, or a repetitive sequence of spiky, architectural *Aloe humilis* (spider aloe) along a windowsill.

If the bathtub is freestanding, a useful little table or storage unit placed next to it could benefit from a small version of a plant such as *Schefflera actinophylla* (Queensland umbrella plant). If the tub is fitted, banish the lotions and potions from one corner and replace them with a plant—just avoid bushy or trailing numbers for this kind of position. Meanwhile, a neatly potted *Haworthia margaritifera* (pearl plant) on one corner of a sink shelf or, even better, a matching pair on each end, creates a lot of impact for a small plant.

While colored fixtures and patterned tiling are making a comeback in bathroom design, most of us still opt for timeless white fittings. In planting terms, this is a good thing. The rich, vibrant greens of foliage plants that suit a bathroom environment really pop against a light-reflecting white backdrop.

BATH & SINK NOOKS

FOCAL-POINT BATHROOM PLANTS

* *Asplenium nidus* (bird's nest fern)
* *Hedera helix* (English ivy)
* *Oncidium* orchids
* *Sansevieria trifasciata* (mother-in-law's tongue)
* *Spathiphyllum wallisii* (peace lily)

This page:
Ferns, such as *Asplenium nidus* (bird's nest fern), are a good choice for a bathroom that has little natural light.

This page:
A pair of humidity-loving *Howea forsteriana* (Kentia palm) placed at either end of a claw-foot tub makes for a truly showstopping display. An *Asplenium nidus* (bird's nest fern) and *Adiantum raddianum* (Delta maidenhair fern) complete the look.

Left:
A selection of miniature succulents and *Hedera helix* (English ivy), all in white containers, add interest to this built-in bathroom storage. The plants will need to be swapped around every two weeks so those on the lower shelf receive their share of natural light.

Below:
Philodendron scandens (heart-leaf philodendron) drapes gently down this bathroom cabinet, softening its hard, angular edges.

SOFTENING HARD LINES

Whether we like it or not, bathrooms can often end up looking or feeling quite clinical and therefore "hard." This is generally due to the typical materials used in bathroom design—namely ceramic, stone, metal, and glass. But plants can soften this impression. Choose those that will softly rustle in any slight breeze. Loose, trailing varieties such as *Epipremnum aureum* (devil's ivy), *Peperomia scandens* 'Variegata' (variegated Cupid peperomia), and *Tradescantia* (wandering Jew) work especially well when draped over shelf edges, tucked into built-in niches, or displayed in hanging planters.

Another benefit of plants is that they are good at reducing noise by absorbing, diffracting, and deflecting sound waves, which is particularly useful in rooms with hard surfaces, such as the bathroom. Positioning plants in a corner or creating a group at different heights—try a *Dracaena fragrans* 'Massangeana' (corn plant) and a *Philodendron bipinnatifidum* (horsehead philodendron)—will give you the maximum noise reduction, and that tinny echo that currently rattles around the space will be a thing of the past.

FIVE GREAT NOISE ABSORBERS
* *Dracaena draco* (dragon tree)
* *Ficus benjamina* (weeping fig)
* *Philodendron bipinnatifidum* (horsehead philodendron)
* *Schefflera arboricola* (dwarf umbrella tree)
* *Spathiphyllum wallisii* (peace lily)

TRAILING PLANTS FOR BATHROOMS
* *Chlorophytum comosum* (spider plant)
* *Epipremnum aureum* (devil's ivy)
* *Hedera helix* (English ivy)
* *Philodendron scandens* (heart-leaf philodendron)
* *Tetrastigma voinierianum* (chestnut vine)

Above left:
Vanda orchids love the warm, damp conditions of the bathroom and look incredibly dramatic suspended from wires, with their roots on display.

Above right:
Both *Tradescantia* (wandering Jew) and *Aloe variegata* (partridge breast aloe), thrive in the damp and humid conditions typical of bathrooms.

OTHER IDEAS

Orchids are particularly fond of the hot, humid conditions in a bathroom and can be a dramatic and colorful addition. *Phalaenopsis* species (moth orchids) are pretty indestructible and widely available, but Ian's current favorites are *Vanda* orchids, which behave like air plants and happily survive unpotted. And the requirement to mist their roots every day will happen anyway in a well-used family bathroom. Because they are so extraordinary, just one can have a huge impact.

Plants with colored or variegated foliage are another good way to introduce an additional design detail into a bright bathroom. Try an *Aglaonema* 'Silver Queen' (Chinese evergreen) or a *Calathea makoyana* (peacock plant).

Choose containers to highlight any accent colors or finishes and to complement or contrast with the bathroom fittings. Use metallic pots to emphasize any brassware, or juxtapose with black planters if the room is totally white. White ceramic pots are the default neutral choice for a bathroom, so select these if you want your plants to do the talking.

Bathrooms often have limited floor space, so you will probably need to look up when positioning plants—think shelves or the tops of cabinets. A display of hanging planters dangling over the bathtub works very well, but make sure they don't hang too low or you will risk banging your head every time you get in and out of the tub.

This page:
Avoid clinical vibes with
some soft green foliage,
such as these *Asparagus
setaceus* (asparagus fern),
Adiantum raddianum (Delta
maidenhair fern), and
Asplenium nidus (bird's nest
fern) on a tiered table.

12
PLANTS FOR BATHING SPACES

Phalaenopsis
Common name:
Moth orchid
Light: Moderate to bright indirect light
Care: This plant tolerates high humidity.
Tips: Cut the stem back to the second notch from the base after flowering to encourage future buds.

Aloe vera
Common name:
Barbados aloe
Light: Bright light
Care: Keep the soil moist.
Tips: Avoid fluctuations in temperature.

Dionaea muscipula
Common name:
Venus fly trap
Light: Moderate to bright indirect light
Care: Use distilled water and never allow the plant to dry out.
Tips: This plant is ideal for terrariums.

Hedera helix
Common name:
English ivy
Light: Bright light
Care: Allow the surface of the soil to dry between waterings.
Tips: This is a great trailing plant that can be trained into different shapes; keep it well pruned.

Aphelandra squarrosa
Common name:
Zebra plant
Light: Bright light
Care: Keep the soil moist.
Tips: Clip off the flower branch after a few days after the bloom fades to encourage future blooms.

Asplenium nidus
Common name:
Bird's nest fern
Light: Moderate indirect light
Care: Water the plant lightly and often.
Tips: Clip off brown fronds with scissors.

Chamaedorea elegans
Common name:
Parlor palm
Light: Low light
Care: Keep the soil moist.
Tips: Mist regularly to increase humidity.

Chlorophytum comosum
Common name:
Spider plant
Light: Moderate to bright light
Care: Keep the soil moist.
Tips: An easy plant to grow and propagate—snip off the "babies" and replant them in a separate pot.

Medinilla magnifica
Common name:
Rose grape
Light: Bright filtered light
Care: This plant enjoys high humidity and moderate watering.
Tips: Prune the plant back to half its size after flowering to promote future blossoms.

Philodendron xanadu
Common name:
None
Light: Moderate light
Care: Allow the soil to dry out between waterings.
Tips: Tuck its aerial roots back into the pot.

Spathiphyllum wallisii
Common name:
Peace lily
Light: Moderate to bright light; tolerates shade
Care: This plant thrives in high humidity. Keep the soil moist.
Tips: Remove flowering stems when the blooms turn green, and keep the leaves clean and polished.

Vanda orchid
Common name:
None
Light: Moderate to bright indirect light
Care: This plant tolerates high humidity.
Tips: Mist daily and avoid letting the roots become soggy.

CHILDREN'S SPACES

It's good to teach children how to nurture a living thing. They enjoy getting their hands dirty, and doing some indoor gardening lets them see how nature works close-up. Choose plants for them that are easy to grow and tend, such as succulents and *Kalanchoe blossfeldiana* (flaming Katy). Another good choice is plants that grow quickly, such as *Lepidium sativum* (garden cress) (see page 125).

Encourage children to grow plants from the seeds they find in some of the fruits or veggies they eat, such as apples, chilies, and avocados. You won't get any sort of meaningful crop, but it's enjoyable to do. See pages 22 and 23 for other edibles that are easy to grow indoors.

Chlorophytum comosum (spider plant), which sprouts "babies" at a rapid rate, and *Maranta leuconeura* (prayer plant), which folds its leaves at night, are fun choices for young children, too, and they also grow quickly and easily. Let them plant a container of small spring bulbs— try *Muscari* (grape hyacinth), *Galanthus* (snowdrop), or *Crocus*—and watch them develop and bloom.

TIP

Remember to teach children good gardening hygiene: Never taste or eat any part of a plant (apart from any edibles, of course!) and always wash their hands after doing any gardening.

Above:
Fun planting containers add extra appeal, such as this LEGO storage head, filled with *Beaucarnea recurvata* (elephant's foot).

Right:
A terrarium becomes even more fun when accessorized with favorite small toys, such as these Schleich animals.

FOR YOUNGER CHILDREN

Left:
Intersperse the books and toys on a child's shelf with some easy-care plants.

Above:
A white wicker basket is given a color boost with spiky *Guzmania* and dramatic *Medinilla magnifica* (rose grape).

Miniature gardens and small trough-style containers with a mixed selection of easy-to-grow plants, such as *Beaucarnea recurvata* (elephant's foot) and *Crassula ovata* (jade plant), are perfect container plants for younger children to look after. The same goes for miniaturized versions of "grownup" plants, such as *Asparagus setaceus* (asparagus fern), *Ficus microcarpa* 'Ginseng' (Indian laurel), and ~~Helxine soleirolii~~ particularly cute in their smaller forms.

Have fun with the plant containers, too. Try out pieces of children's paraphernalia, such as pencil pots, melamine cups, candy tins, and so on. There are a plethora of quirky, cute, kitsch, and humorous pots on the market—whether brightly decorated with faces, or in the shapes of animals—which all slot extremely well into children's rooms. A lovely but also rather impactful idea is to incorporate a few of the child's small toys, figurines, or models alongside the plants, to capture the imagination.

Safety is, of course, a key consideration when introducing plants into a younger child's room. Obviously, avoid spiky cacti as well as plants that are potentially toxic if ingested, such as *Spathiphyllum wallisii* (peace lily), *Sansevieria trifasciata* (mother-in-law's tongue), and *Epipremnum aureum* (devil's ivy). Think carefully, too, about where to position them so they are out of reach or tucked away where they won't be easily knocked over.

TIP

With very young children, use planters made from plastic or metal—rather than ceramic or terracotta—as they are both lighter and more robust when being handled.

GROWING GARDEN CRESS

This project for a young child is even more exciting if you use a container with a face, so you are effectively growing its hair.

* Place some soggy paper towels in your pot of choice.
* Sprinkle in the *Lepidium sativum* (garden cress) seeds and put the planted pot in a shady spot.
* When the seeds begin to sprout, move the pot to a windowsill. The cress will be ready to harvest after a week or so.

Right:
A neat line of different-shape cacti planted in sophisticated containers works well on an older child's desk.

Opposite page:
Sansevieria cylindrica and *Asparagus setaceus* (asparagus fern) are handsome and virtually indestructible—useful qualities in a teenager's room.

FOR OLDER CHILDREN

When children grow up and turn from tweens into teens, having their own space becomes more and more important to them. As a parent, you'll want to make sure you don't stifle their attempts at self-expression by trying to impose your taste on them. Instead, you need to work with them.

Tweens and teens tend to gravitate toward things that feel a bit more grownup and edgy. In plant terms, this translates into all the varieties that have something quirky about them, even verging on the macabre. Think of those plants that have a bit of a story to tell: *Tillandsia* (air plant), any number of cool-looking cacti, or the various members of the fern family, which date back to prehistoric times.

By this age, your child is likely to have accumulated quite a lot of stuff, so a good approach is to choose plants that can be sprinkled in among their books

and trinkets. This is generation smartphone, and older children are well versed in what looks good. Photogenic shelfie-style arrangements will appeal to this crowd.

Plants with variegated or colorful foliage, such as *Maranta leuconeura* var. *erythroneura* (herringbone plant) and *Begonia rex* (King Begonia), can be used as a subtle way of introducing color into an older child's room. Flowering plants will probably appeal more if they are peculiar or idiosyncratic in some way. The bromeliads, such as *Guzmania lingulata* (scarlet star plant) and *Vriesea splendens* (flaming sword), will work well. If something bolder is wanted, consider a larger specimen plant, such as an architectural *Howea forsteriana* (Kentia palm). The added bonus of all these plants is that they are pretty sturdy and good-looking.

TIP
....
Succulents are brilliant starter plants for children of all ages. Compact in size, they can take a fair amount of neglect, if, for example, they are accidentally left unwatered for a few weeks.

Left:
Cacti that can cope with missing a watering every now and then are always a good choice for an older child's bedroom.

Right:
Displayed like an animal skull, a prehistoric-looking *Tillandsia* (air plant) often appeals to teenagers because of its unusual, somewhat quirky nature.

QUIRKY PLANTS FOR OLDER KIDS

* *Codiaeum variegatum* var. *pictum* (croton). The different hybrids have dramatically vibrant foliage with variously shaped leaves. They need a bit of care, so these are best for your budding horticulturist.
* Desert cacti. The sheer variety of shapes and sizes, and the fact that they are pretty much unkillable, gives them an edge.
* *Dionaea muscipula* (Venus fly trap). These are the spectacular-looking carnivores of the plant world.
* *Lithops* (living stone). As well as really looking like small stones, these produce surprising, dramatic flowers in fall.
* *Tillandsia* (air plant). These plants are amazing because of their quirk of quite literally living on air.

As for containers and where to position them, the same rules apply here as to everywhere else in the home, but let your child take the lead. Would she like subtle, sophisticated planters or prefer something a little more colorful and unusual? Does she want to position the plant in a spot that commands immediate attention or would she prefer smaller varieties that can be subtly accommodated among their other possessions? Is she keen on the idea of an on-trend terrarium?

As teenagers have a tendency to be a bit on the clumsy side, make sure their plants are placed on a stable surface or tucked safely out of the way from any accidental knocks. Think toward the back of a shelf or desk rather than at the front, or, if they are standing on the floor, positioned in a corner.

Above all, be realistic. It's probably best to choose varieties of plants that can take a fair bit of neglect in case the "Keep Out" sign goes on the door and you aren't allowed access to water any plants for a few weeks at a time . . .

TIP
....
Why not get your older child to design and plant a terrarium scheme? The following plants are all good choices for terrariums: *Crassula ovata* (jade plant), *Tillandsia* (air plant), and the various small forms of fern, cacti, and succulents.

12
PLANTS FOR CHILDREN'S SPACES

Gerbera jamesonii
Common name: Barberton daisy
Light: Moderate to bright light
Care: Keep the soil moist while in bloom but let it dry out slightly afterward.
Tips: Remove dead flowers to encourage blooming for as long as possible.

Codiaeum variegatum
Common name: Croton
Light: Moderate to bright light
Care: Keep the soil slightly moist.
Tips: Prune the top when the plant becomes tall, and root it like a stem tip cutting.

Maranta leuconeura
Common name: Prayer plant
Light: Moderate light
Care: This plant enjoys high humidity; keep the soil moist.
Tips: Trim the plant back to keep its shape and promote new growth.

Philodendron xanadu
Common name: None
Light: Moderate light
Care: Allow the soil to dry out between waterings.
Tips: Tuck its aerial roots back into the pot.

Dionaea muscipula
Common name:
Venus fly trap
Light: Moderate to bright indirect light
Care: Use distilled water and never allow the plant to dry out.
Tips: This plant is ideal for terrariums.

Echeveria elegans
Common name:
Mexican gem
Light: Bright light
Care: Keep the soil slightly moist.
Tips: Remove the offshoots and propagate them to prevent the pot from becoming overcrowded.

Kalanchoe blossfeldiana
Common name:
Flaming Katy
Light: Moderate to bright indirect light
Care: Water only when the soil is dry.
Tips: Pinch off blooms after the flowers fade to preserve the look of the plant.

Lithops
Common name:
Living stone
Light: Moderate to bright light
Care: Water the soil lightly in spring and fall.
Tips: Keep the plant dry in summer and winter to follow its natural growth cycle.

Schlumbergera truncata
Common name:
Christmas cactus
Light: Indirect light
Care: This plant tolerates high humidity. Keep the soil well drained.
Tips: To prevent flowers from dropping, avoid over-watering, under-watering, and other forms of stress.

Tillandsia cyanea
Common name:
Pink quill
Light: Bright light
Care: Mist the plant twice weekly to keep the soil moist.
Tips: Keep the plant cool in winter to encourage spring blooms.

Tradescantia fluminensis
Common name:
Wandering Jew
Light: Bright to moderate light
Care: Water thoroughly, and allow the surface of the soil to dry out between waterings.
Tips: Mist frequently.

Vanda orchid
Common name:
None
Light: Moderate to bright indirect light
Care: This plant tolerates high humidity; be sure to mist daily.
Tips: Avoid letting the roots become soggy.

WORKING SPACES

More and more of us are spending at least some part of our working lives doing our jobs from home—whether full-time, part-time, or the odd day here and there. This means that an office is now a more frequent feature of our homes than ever before. It can be as simple and straightforward as a desk tucked into a discreet corner of the house or a fully equipped room, complete with reference library and all the latest tech gadgets.

Since a home office is a working space, it obviously needs to be practical, with all the resources you need for the job easily accessible. But it should also be inspirational—somewhere that pushes you to be creative and to do your best work. With that in mind, what could be more pleasant than looking up from your computer for a screen break and feasting your eyes upon some carefully chosen plants?

Color theory classifies green as the color of nature, which isn't exactly rocket science. However, it is the anecdotal associations given to the color that are interesting in this context.

TIP

Houseplants are much more than eye candy. There are a number of positive psychological reasons for introducing some greenery into an office zone.

Green is perceived as the color of calm, and it is believed to relieve stress—just what you need when under pressure from a work deadline. It is also considered to be the color of stability and endurance; perhaps it will help you keep plugging away at that project. Historically, it has been associated with wisdom, intelligence, and confidence—all qualities we would like in our working selves.

People also associate green with good health, so it's interesting that as well as there being all the positive mood benefits linked with the color green, plants in an office will bring actual health benefits—but more about that on page 137.

So, what more excuses do you need? Start greening up your home office now.

GREEN PSYCHOLOGY

In the world of psychology, the color green makes you feel:

* Positive
* Calm
* Relaxed
* Uplifted
* Refreshed

* Stable
* Clever
* Confident
* Tranquil
* Balanced

This page:
A single specimen plant, such as this stately *Carnegiea gigantea* (saguaro), can create all the impact you need in a room.

This page:
Choose smaller varieties of your preferred plants for a desktop scheme, such as this collection of ferns, containing *Athyrium* (lady fern), *Didymochlaena truncatula* (mahogany fern), and *Pteris dentata* 'Stramina' (toothed brake).

This page:
Dotting small succulents
and cacti among reference
books and stationery adds
visual interest without
taking up too much space.

Left:
A serving cart makes a portable plant container. Here, *Spathiphyllum wallisii* (peace lily), known for its pollutant-filtering properties, has been added to an assortment.

Below:
A living wall—style planter is space-saving and an interesting way of introducing plants into a small office. This one is planted with a mixture of ferns and succulents.

HEALTH

We discussed the health benefits of having plants in the home earlier in the book (see page 14), but let's explore it a bit more here in the context of an office space. Most of the relevant research has focused on the benefits of indoor plants in large corporate offices, but it stands to reason that many of those findings also apply to a domestic office space.

Ian and the team he directs at London's Indoor Garden Design have since investigated much of the research on the positive effects of plants in an office environment, and they have concluded that introducing just one plant near your work station can start to bring about beneficial changes. It can reduce feelings of anxiety and stress and also help to improve concentration, particularly for those of us whose work is computer-based.

An especially significant study done in 2009 at the University of Technology in Sydney, Australia, came to the conclusion that it is highly probable that all plants absorb toxins from the air as part of their biological processes. The kinds of toxins we are talking about are those pesky volatile organic compounds (VOCs; see page 14 for more information). In essence, these are the invisible pollutants released from the many common man-made products we all have in our homes, such as carpets and cleaning products. If we have a home office, there are additional VOCs from computers, printers, and other common office essentials.

My dad has always been convinced that the humble spider plant (*Chlorophytum comosum*) is a good absorber of computer emissions. The rest of the family dismissed the theory, but it turns out he has a point: *Chlorophytum* plants are particularly good at processing environmental pollutants.

TIP
....
Adding plants to your office as air filters makes sense in terms of your health as well as aesthetics.

HEALTHY HOME OFFICE PLANTS
* *Aglaonema modestum* (Chinese evergreen)
* *Anthurium scherzerianum* (flamingo flower)
* *Chlorophytum comosum* (spider plant)
* *Dracaena fragrans* 'Janet Craig' (corn plant)
* *Epipremnum aureum* (devil's ivy)
* *Ficus benjamina* (weeping fig)
* *Philodendron scandens* (heart-leaf philodendron)
* *Spathiphyllum wallisii* (peace lily)

DESKS

A desk is usually the main focus of an office zone. It is where you sit to work and where, no doubt, your computer is set up. It also offers another surface with planting potential. As you will see the plants on your desk close-up, small in this situation really is beautiful. A couple of well-chosen *Aloe* and *Echeveria* living among your paperwork, or a trailing *Philodendron scandens* (heart-leaf philodendron) spilling over the side of the desk, will create a dramatic focal point. And since desk space is likely to be at a premium, succulents are generally an appropriate choice because they are slow-growing.

Be inventive with your plant containers, perhaps using an old desk organizer, pen pots, or a trash bin. Look for containers with finishes in light-industrial materials such as galvanized zinc, enamel, or mesh, or create DIY pots wrapped in brown paper, string, or newspaper for a quirky touch.

Whichever look you go for, just make sure the container is waterproof or can be made to be so, since the last thing you need is an accidental leak onto your work or computer. If you tend to be a little clumsy, a group of plants in a self-contained trough or planter works well. On the other hand, individually potted plants give you the flexibility to move them out of the way whenever you need a bit more desk space.

Home office desks are often positioned in front of or close to a window, so you will need to take that into account when selecting your plants, making sure they can cope with the amount of light and its intensity.

Some of the design tricks covered elsewhere in this book can also be called upon for the desk. Neat rows of the same variety work well, as does a display that focuses on foliage colors. Because you will look at them close-up, consider also the intricate shapes of small plant specimens, such as the various cacti or *Aloe*. Last but by no means least, the trusty terrarium is a very useful, tidy, and compact solution for a desk-friendly design.

Above:
A self-contained trough ensures that a collection of plants, like these *Beaucarnea recurvata* (elephant's foot), doesn't take up too much space on a desk.

Right:
Place a restful green display in your line of sight. *Sansevieria trifasciata* var. *laurentii* (variegated snake plant) is compact, slow-growing, and tolerant of all degrees of light, shade, and heat.

TINY PLANTS FOR CLOSE-UPS

* *Aloe variegata* (partridge breast aloe)
* *Crassula muscosa* 'Variegata'
* *Echeveria secunda* var. *glauca* (glaucous echeveria)
* *Echinopsis rhodotricha* (sea-urchin cactus)
* *Tillandsia* (air plant)

Far left:
Bushy and trailing plants
look particularly good
when displayed on a
shelving unit.

Left:
Use individually potted
plants as spacers in order
to break up solid rows of
reference books.

Shelves, as we know, are very useful for featuring plants. Such displays work best when they are kept simple and bold: Try using a few individually potted plants as decorative spacers to break up solid rows of reference books. You could even employ a plant as a bookend.

If the shelves are deep enough, use the area in front of the books to arrange a line of plants. This is also a good way to camouflage unattractive box folders or magazine files. Create an indoor view with a grouped arrangement on a shelf at eye level. For strategic placement, aim for the height you look at when glancing up from your computer screen. Trailing plants look dramatic draped over the edge of shelves and work particularly well on a tall shelving unit.

No room on your desk for plants? Then be bold and choose a tall, architectural specimen that can stand guard over you while you work. Alternatively, put a plant stand, a stepstool, or some library steps to good use as a way of giving medium-size plants more presence. Employ the top tray of a serving cart or soften the functional lines of a file cabinet by placing a cluster of three *Sansevieria trifasciata* 'Hahnii' (bird's nest sansevieria) or five different *Echeveria* on top.

If there just isn't a free flat surface in your home office, it's still possible to introduce some green—with hanging planters. The trailing varieties that look good draped over shelf edges, such as *Trandescantia* (wandering Jew) and *Rhipsalis baccifera* (mistletoe cactus), will also work here. And there is nothing more fabulously retro—and therefore chic—than a group of three *Chlorophytum comosum* (spider plants), encased in macramé pot holders hanging at different heights over the corner of your desk.

SHELVES & OTHER SPACES

HIDING A HOME OFFICE

If your home office is part of a larger space, you can screen it off from the rest of the room with a row of tall plants. *Howea forsteriana* (Kentia palm), *Dracaena fragrans* (corn plant), *Yucca elephantipes* (spineless yucca), or, if it is a bright room, *Ficus benjamina* (weeping fig) or *Euphorbia tirucalli* (pencil tree) all fit the bill with their dramatic outlines. Plus, they have the additional benefit of filtering pollutants from the air.

12
PLANTS
FOR WORKING
SPACES

Howea forsteriana
Common name:
Kentia palm
Light: Low light
Care: Keep the soil moist.
Tips: This plant is
relatively slow-growing
and rarely needs
repotting.

Aechmea fasciata
Common name:
Urn plant
Light: Bright light
Care: Lightly water the
roots, and replenish
the water in the plant's
reservoir when it dries out.
Tips: Epsom salts and
bright light can be used to
induce a pinkish-orange
bloom in spring.

Crassula ovata 'Gollum'
Common name:
Gollum jade plant
Light: Bright light
Care: This plant tolerates
high humidity. Keep the
soil well drained.
Tips: Plenty of light and
fertilizer improves the
leaf color.

Echeveria secunda
Common name:
None
Light: Bright light
Care: This plant tolerates
high humidity. Keep the
soil well drained.
Tips: Pinch off the blooms
to preserve the appearance
of the rosettes.

Araucaria heterophylla
Common name:
Norfolk Island pine
Light: Bright light
Care: Keep the soil
slightly moist.
Tips: Turn the plant
regularly to promote even
growth, and trim only
lower branches.

Beaucarnea recurvata
Common name:
Elephant's foot
Light: Bright light
Care: This plant enjoys
high humidity and should
be allowed to dry out
between waterings.
Tips: Keep its leaves clean
with a damp cloth.

Calathea makoyana
Common name:
Peacock plant
Light: Bright indirect
light
Care: This plant enjoys
high humidity, and the soil
should be kept moist.
Tips: Mist the plant daily.

Chlorophytum comosum
Common name:
Spider plant
Light: Moderate to
bright light
Care: Keep the soil moist.
Tips: An easy plant to grow
and propagate—snip off
the "babies" and replant
them in a separate pot.

Euphorbia tirucalli
Common name:
Pencil tree
Light: Full sunlight
Care: Water three times a
week over the summer, and
keep the soil well drained.
Tips: This plant needs
very little care, but prune
if it becomes too big.

Ficus microcarpa 'Ginseng'
Common name:
Indian laurel
Light: Bright indirect
light
Care: Keep the plant
moist, and mist regularly.
Tips: Prune regularly to
retain the plant's shape;
for every six to eight leaves
that grow, prune two back.

Monstera deliciosa
Common name:
Swiss cheese plant
Light: Moderate indirect
light
Care: Allow the soil to dry
out between waterings.
Tips: Secure the plant's
aerial roots close to the
base of the plant on the
surface of the soil.

Spathiphyllum wallisii
Common name:
Peace lily
Light: Moderate to
bright light; tolerates
shade
Care: This plant thrives in
high humidity. Keep the
soil moist.
Tips: Remove flowering
stems when the blooms
turn green, and keep the
leaves clean and polished.

CONNECTING SPACES

In design terms, the entryway and staircase are no longer afterthoughts but rather the spaces where you can set the whole style tone of your home. With that in mind, these areas really lend themselves to interesting indoor plants. Your entryway is the link between the outdoors and the indoors, and it's where you greet your guests, which makes it a logical place to introduce some houseplants if you're intent on greening up your home.

It almost goes without saying that the key thing to remember is to choose plants that can cope with the decreased light levels usually found in entryways. It also helps if they can handle any drafts coming in through the front door, and you should really aim for plants that stay compact, simply because they are suited so much better to a limited space. Harness plants such as *Sansevieria trifasciata* var. *laurentii* (variegated snake plant), *Zamioculcas zamiifolia* (ZZ plant), and *Dracaena fragrans* 'Massangeana' (corn plant) to create a dramatic mood. If you prefer a slightly softer ambiance, try *Tradescantia zebrina* (silver inch plant) or *Tolmiea menziesii* (piggyback plant).

The entryway is also a brilliant space to experiment with seasonal planting and color. In winter, try a container filled with *Cyclamen persicum* (Persian cyclamen), miniature *Ilex* (holly), and *Hedera* (ivy) plants, or even a sequence of tiny *Pinus* (pine) trees. Meanwhile, a bowl of scented bulbs such as *Hyacinthus* (hyacinth), *Narcissus,* or *Primula* (primrose) will, quite literally, bring spring into your home.

As for the question of where to position your plants, a series of one plant per pot per step on a flight of stairs draws the eye up, while a neat grouping of three or five different-size plants clustered on a sideboard can really make a statement. In a small space, symmetry can work extremely well, so try bookending a pair of matching plants on either side of a console. If you have the room, place a low bench or table against the wall and use this to support a row of plants with similar foliage.

It is especially important to rotate any houseplants regularly to ensure they have even access to natural light—no matter how limited it is—which will help them grow evenly and encourage fullness. You will also need to move the pots from time to time to clean around them. With these considerations in mind, choose lightweight planters—think wicker and plastic over ceramic and terracotta—for easy portability.

This page:
An informal row of
attractive plants makes
an entryway particularly
welcoming. From left:
Aglaonema modestum (Chinese
evergreen), *Pteris dentata*
'Stramina' (toothed
brake), *Stromanthe sanguinea*
'Triostar,' *Codiaeum
variegatum* var. *pictum* 'Petra'
(petra croton), *Calathea
makoyana* (peacock plant),
Dracaena fragrans Deremensis
Group 'Lemon Lime,'
and *Beaucarnea recurvata*
(elephant's foot).

ROBUST HALL & STAIRCASE PLANTS

All these plants can take a bash, a draft, and not much light.

✻ *Aglaonema modestum* (Chinese evergreen)

✻ *Aspidistra elatior* (cast-iron plant)

✻ *Beaucarnea recurvata* (elephant's foot)

✻ *Crassula ovata* (jade plant)

✻ *Dracaena fragrans* (corn plant)

✻ *Howea forsteriana* (Kentia palm)

✻ *Platycerium bifurcatum* (staghorn fern)

✻ *Sansevieria trifasciata* (mother-in-law's tongue)

✻ *Soleirolia soleirolii* (mind-your-own-business)

✻ *Yucca elephantipes* (spineless yucca)

✻ *Zamioculcas zamiifolia* (ZZ plant)

Below left:
Putting a small plant like a fern somewhere unexpected, such as hanging from a coat hook, greatly increases its impact.

Below right:
The turn in a staircase is put to good use with the addition of a slim *Dracaena fragrans* Deremensis Group 'Yellow Stripe' (corn plant).

TIP
....
Zamioculcas zamiifolia (ZZ plant) and *Sansevieria trifasciata* (mother-in-law's tongue) are Ian's perfect plants for staircases. They are both unbelievably hardy, stay compact, and can cope with the lack of light.

Below left:
A dramatic display of hanging *Vanda* orchids in this period entryway is complemented by a stairway path of *Zamioculcas zamiifolia* (ZZ plant).

Below right:
Give interest to the side of a staircase with some textural plants. Here, *Platycerium bifurcatum* (staghorn fern) and *Rhipsalis baccifera* (mistletoe cactus) drape down through the spindles, and a basket of palms sits below.

STAIRCASES

The staircase is often a missed design opportunity. It gets an enormous amount of traffic, so it seems an oversight that we don't always make better use of it for expressing our taste preferences.

While edge-to-edge carpeted stairs don't easily lend themselves to rows of potted plants, stairways with a central runner, or polished or painted wooden stairs, are the perfect frameworks for certain plants. Stairs painted in a fail-safe modernist monochrome, whether black or white, provide an excellent backdrop to what are often the deep foliage hues of foyer-appropriate plants. Think of how green sings when positioned against these colors and you will understand how well they offset plants. Varieties with strong foliage shades that would work in this context include *Zamioculcas zamiifolia* (ZZ plant), *Sansevieria trifasciata* (mother-in-law's tongue), and *Crassula ovata* (jade plant).

While a simple scheme of one plant per pot per step—or maybe every other step, depending on the scale and height of both the plant and the staircase—is quite effective, there are other ways

This page:
This narrow planter nestled in against the stair spindles has been planted with *Beaucarnea recurvata* (elephant's foot), which will gently ripple in any breeze. Individual pots of *Sansevieria trifasciata* var. *laurentii* (variegated snake plant) look very smart lined up one behind the other on the stairs.

to look at styling a stairway. Try placing some trailing plants such as *Rhipsalis baccifera* (mistletoe cactus), *Rhoicissus rhomboidea* (glossy forest grape), and *Tetrastigma voinierianum* (chestnut vine) alongside the spindles, so that you can get them to drape through the gaps. A narrow trough or planter set against the banister on a landing area can allow you to introduce several plants into a smaller space. Again, if the banister has spindles, you can add some trailing varieties to the mix to drop down over the edge.

You can also put the draping technique to good use on the narrow niches, ledges, and windowsills that so often appear in a stairwell. Positioning some trailing plants so that they cascade over a ledge is an attractive design device that can make an interesting feature of an otherwise ignored spot. An alternative is to create a group of small pots on a narrow windowsill with appropriately scaled plants. Like most staircase ideas, it is simple yet powerful. Another often overlooked location is the angle of a top or half-landing. These corners

can provide a great setting for a plant, both framing and protecting it.

Stairway-appropriate plants are often foliage-based, so if you would like to introduce some strong colors or patterns to the space, look to your planters. The kinds of repetitive line schemes that work well on a staircase can look even punchier if you have the plants in interesting containers.

Above left:
This position is perfect for troughs planted with multiple *Codiaeum variegatum* (croton), as they need plenty of light to keep them looking their best.

Above right:
Positioning trailing plants, such as these *Hedera helix* (English ivy), so that they cascade over a ledge makes a feature of an otherwise ignored spot.

ENTRYWAYS

Entryways and hallways are usually narrow, requiring compact plants, but that doesn't mean they can't have any impact. A tall, thin architectural plant such as a mature *Euphorbia tirucalli* (pencil tree) or a *Dracaena fragrans* 'Compacta' (dragon tree) can be truly striking. Always choose a pot that's in proportion to the room, since the last thing you need in a restricted space is a huge urn that everyone constantly bumps into.

Though a single bold plant is the straightforward option, an original touch is to pop a plant somewhere unexpected—in a neat hanging planter off a coat hook or dangling from a newel post or a picture rail, for example. A few tiny specimens dotted along the top of a tall cabinet or a radiator cover can also be fun. For the latter, choose plants like succulents and cacti that don't mind warm, dry air and variations in heat. And, rather than hanging a picture or a mirror, how about a wall planter instead? Have a horizontal or vertical line of single planters or buy a specialty design that will allow you to plant a mini living wall (see page 59). To draw the eye through the length of the space, add a green path of the same type of plant at even intervals next to the wall (so it isn't a tripping hazard).

Console tables and shoe cubbies are a useful addition if your entryway is wide enough to take one—not only as a dumping ground for general family detritus, but as a surface for plants. Position your plants at the end that gets the most light coming through door panes or side lights.

Left:
Thin, tall, and architectural, this *Euphorbia tirucalli* (pencil tree) makes a striking addition to a narrow foyer.

Above:
Take advantage of a console table as a display surface. This *Zamioculcas zamiifolia* (ZZ plant) and *Platycerium bifurcatum* (staghorn fern) both cope well with the lower light levels often found in entryways.

ADDING COLOR TO AN ENTRYWAY
If your entryway has reasonable light, choose plants with vibrant foliage colors or strikingly exotic flowers, such as:
✽ *Anthurium scherzerianum* (flamingo flower)
✽ *Calathea makoyana* (peacock plant)
✽ *Cardiaeum variegatum* var. *pictum* 'Petra' (petra croton)
✽ *Guzmania lingulata* (scarlet star plant)
✽ *Vriesea splendens* (flaming sword)

12

PLANTS FOR CONNECTING SPACES

Aglaonema
Common name: Chinese evergreen
Light: Moderate light
Care: Keep the soil slightly moist.
Tips: Pinch off new leaves to encourage bushiness.

Aspidistra elatior
Common name: Cast-iron plant
Light: Low light
Care: This plant needs only moderate watering.
Tips: Repot every three years to refresh the soil.

Philodendron xanadu
Common name: None
Light: Moderate light
Care: Allow the soil to dry out between waterings.
Tips: Tuck its aerial roots back into the pot.

Sansevieria trifasciata
Common name: Mother-in-law's tongue
Light: Moderate to bright light
Care: This plant doesn't require much water.
Tips: It's one of the easiest houseplants to look after! Keep the leaves clean.

Dracaena marginata
Common name:
Madagascar dragon tree
Light: Moderate
indirect light
Care: This plant needs
only moderate watering.
Tips: Keep the leaves well
pruned to control the
plant's height.

Ficus elastica
Common name:
Rubber plant
Light: Bright to
moderate light
Care: Keep the soil
slightly moist and do not
over-water.
Tips: Keep the leaves
clean and shiny, and avoid
placing the plant in drafts
or cold rooms.

Howea forsteriana
Common name:
Kentia palm
Light: Low light
Care: Keep the soil moist.
Tips: This plant is
relatively slow-growing
and rarely needs
repotting.

Peperomia caperata
Common name:
Emerald ripple
Light: Low to moderate
light
Care: Allow the soil to dry
out between waterings.
Tips: Over-watering is
about the only thing that
will damage this plant.

Epipremnum aureum
Common name:
Devil's ivy
Light: Moderate to
bright light
Care: This plant enjoys
high humidity. Keep the
soil moist, but do not
over-water.
Tips: Prune twice a year
to keep the plant looking
bushy and full.

Spathiphyllum wallisii
Common name:
Peace lily
Light: Moderate to
bright light; tolerates
shade
Care: This plant thrives in
high humidity. Keep the
soil moist.
Tips: Remove flowering
stems when the blooms
turn green, and keep the
leaves clean and polished.

Yucca
Common name: None
Light: Bright to
moderate light
Care: This plant does not
need much water, so keep it
relatively dry.
Tips: Don't let this plant
get too cold.

Zamioculcas zamiifolia
Common name:
ZZ plant
Light: Low light
Care: This plant doesn't
require much water.
Tips: This tough plant can
cope with neglect.

THE BASICS

LIGHT

The basic building blocks for every plant's survival are light, water, and carbon dioxide. Our school biology classes may remind us why they're crucial: A plant "drinks" water, "breathes" carbon dioxide, and harnesses light to photosynthesize, using the chloroplasts (which give a plant its green color) in its leaf cells to convert light energy into sugar, or, in other words, plant food. Oxygen is a by-product of this process. If any element is missing, the plant cannot make food and will die.

Though the brightness of light needed by each plant varies, they do all need light to some degree for at least 12 hours a day in the growing season. When deciding which houseplants to have where, take into account not only the amount of light they require but also the light levels in each room. Observe where the light comes in and when, where any shadows form, and how the light moves and changes in intensity during the day. In general, light levels are reduced the closer you are to the ceiling, which is worth noting when choosing plants for cabinet tops or hanging plant displays.

It's said that clean, dust-free windows may raise light levels by as much as 10 percent. Though we haven't tested this scientifically, it's worth bearing in mind.

TIP

The paler the color of the walls and ceiling, the more natural light is reflected around the room; the opposite is true for dark colors, which absorb light. Keep this in mind when you're selecting and positioning plants.

GUIDING LIGHT

This is a rough guide to which light conditions suit which types of plants. To be on the safe side, check the requirements of your chosen plants before you buy.

* **Full Shade** No plant will survive perpetually low light levels.
* **Semi-shade (entryways & shady spots)** Choose hardy foliage plants such as *Aspidistra elatior* (cast-iron plant), *Sansevieria trifasciata* (mother-in-law's tongue), *Zamioculcas zamiifolia* (ZZ plant), and compact-growing *Dracaena*.
* **Bright (average living room light)** This suits nearly all plants. Try palms, flowering plants such as orchids and bulbs, and foliage plants with variegated leaves.
* **Sunlight (bright windowsills)** Choose cacti and succulents, herbs, and members of the *Ficus* (fig) family.
* **Full sunlight (south-facing windowsills)** Most houseplants dislike being in direct sunlight, especially in summer, as the sun will burn their leaves.

DANGER SIGNS

When there is too little light:
* Leaves start to yellow
* Variegated leaves turn completely green
* Leaves drop
* Potting soil stays damp and doesn't dry out as quickly as expected; the plant may become waterlogged if you continue to water

When there is too much light:
* Leaves wilt
* Leaves suffer from brown tips or brown scorched patches
* Potting soil dries out too quickly

This page:
Flowering indoor plants, such as the *Cattleya* orchid and the taller *Phalaenopsis* orchids, need plenty of light to ensure they thrive and produce flowers.

This page:
A portable watering can with a long, narrow spout is an essential piece of gear for the indoor gardener.

WHEN & HOW TO WATER

In caring for our houseplants, we are most likely to slip up with the watering. Fact: All plants need water to some degree in order to survive. If a plant dries out, it becomes weak and therefore prone to pests and disease. Ditto if it's too wet. There are no hard-and-fast rules about the frequency of watering—it depends on the plant type, its size, and the time of the year, among other things.

For all houseplants (excluding orchids, air plants, succulents, and cacti), water by carefully and gently pouring water into the gap between the foliage and the potting soil until the space between the top of the soil and the lip of the container is filled with water. Using a small, long-spouted watering can is the easiest way to do this. (Try to avoid getting water on the leaves and flowers, as this can damage them.) Let the plant stand for up to ten minutes to allow excess water to drain through the soil. If there is still water sitting on the top, carefully pour it off. There is a difference between keeping the soil moist—which is what most plants want—and wet, which can lead to waterlogging and root rot.

Plants need water more often in the spring and summer than in winter. The general rule of thumb is that if the top of the soil looks dry and powdery, you need to water.

TIP
....
It is best to use tepid (room temperature) water. Never leave a houseplant standing in water.

HAPPY PLANT HOLIDAYS

It is generally safe to leave your houseplants unattended for up to two weeks. However, if they are left for any longer—especially during the summer growing season—you are taking the risk of plant apocalypse when you return. Failing a friendly plant sitter, there are a few things you can do to avert disaster:

✱ Group plants together in a cool spot, away from direct sunlight, to raise the humidity levels around them. Even if you have a plant sitter, grouping your plants together will help them do their job more efficiently.

✱ Water all your plants thoroughly just before your departure, but don't leave them standing in water, such as in a bathtub.

✱ In winter, leave the heat on. The ideal temperature is between 64 and 70°F (18–21°C)—a.k.a. "room temperature"—but houseplants can manage temps as low as 59°F (15°C).

✱ Keep an eye out for tech. The development of app-enabled watering systems is underway, letting you to water your plants remotely, no matter where you are.

DANGER SIGNS
When there is too much water:
✱ Young and old leaves fall at the same time
✱ Leaves develop brown patches
✱ Plant generally looks a bit moldy
✱ Plant develops root rot, with mushy-looking dark roots that can start to smell

When there is too little water:
✱ Leaf edges turn brown and dry
✱ Leaves wilt and look limp
✱ Lower leaves curl and turn yellow
✱ Leaves may become translucent

PLANT CARE

Indoor plants are surprisingly low-maintenance, and with a little regular love and attention, they will thrive. Here's what you need to do and when.

General pointers
All plants need light, water, food, and warmth—a bit like people, really—but they vary in the amounts they need, and that's where you have to do some research. If you treat different types of houseplants the same way, sooner or later you will run into problems. Broadly speaking, though, there are a few rules that apply to them all.

Generic general-purpose potting soil is fine to use across the board; although there are specialty houseplant mixes available, they're not essential. A liquid feed specifically for houseplants is, however, no bad thing. Use it every couple of weeks during the growing season (mid-spring to early fall) but never in winter, and make sure you follow the instructions on the packet, as the requirements for different plants will vary. You will also need to reduce the watering of all plants in winter, when they need a rest period, but take care not to let them dry out when you turn on the central heat (see also page 161).

Get into the habit of regularly checking both sides of the leaves and the potting soil for any signs of pests and disease. If you catch any problems at an early stage, you will be able to eradicate them more easily (see pages 166–168).

With the exception of succulents and cacti, all houseplants hate a hot, dry environment, so don't put them near a radiator. Orchids and ferns love the humidity of a bathroom or a kitchen. No plant, however, likes being in a draft.

To avoid stressing your plants, don't move them around too much. Light levels, humidity, and temperature can vary a lot from room to room, and a change in these can badly affect a plant.

Pruning
Pruning is not essential for the good maintenance of houseplants. The only reason you would have to prune is if you need to check a plant's growth or if it is becoming a bit misshapen or leggy, which can be an issue with *Ficus* plants especially.

If pruning is necessary, do it either just at the start or right at the end of the growing season. Also, be gentle on your plant—prune just enough to keep it in shape, and always stop above a bud, no matter how much growth you are removing.

WHAT'S THE PROBLEM?
If plants aren't looking their best, the cause may be easily remedied. For more serious problems, see pages 166–168.

* **Brown leaf tips** Not enough water or too much light
* **Yellow/brown leaves** Insufficient or too much light
* **Flat, brown spots** Too much light or too much water
* **Pale leaves** Too much light or not enough water
* **Drooping leaves** The environment is too dry or too hot
* **Falling leaves** Over- or under-watering or a sudden change in temperature
* **Lopsided growth** The plant is growing to the light, and the pot is not being turned regularly enough

PETS & HOUSEPLANTS

We all know that some garden plants, such as *Atropa belladonna* (deadly nightshade) and *Digitalis* (foxglove), are poisonous to both people and pets, but, sadly, some of the fabulous houseplants that we have namedropped in this book don't get on so well with our furry friends either. If eaten by your cat or dog, they may cause breathing difficulties, skin and stomach problems, a swollen tongue, vomiting, diarrhea, and, in the worst case, seizures, a coma, and even death.

This list of plants that are **not** pet-friendly is by no means comprehensive, so before making any plant purchases, double-check with your garden center or veterinarian for compatibility. Remember that it's better to be safe than sorry.

* *Aglaonema modestum* (Chinese evergreen)
* *Aloe vera* (Barbados aloe)
* *Anthurium scherzerianum* (flamingo flower)
* *Asparagus setaceus* (asparagus fern)
* *Begonia rex* (King Begonia)
* *Crassula ovata* (jade plant)
* *Cyclamen persicum* (Persian cyclamen)
* *Dieffenbachia* (dumb cane)
* *Dracaena fragrans* (corn plant)
* *Epipremnum aureum* (devil's ivy)
* *Euphorbia tirucalli* (pencil tree)
* *Fatsia japonica* (Japanese aralia)
* *Ficus* plants, particularly *F. benjamina* (weeping fig)
* *Hedera helix* (English ivy)
* *Hippeastrum* (amaryllis)
* *Hyacinthus* (hyacinth)
* *Monstera deliciosa* (Swiss cheese plant)
* *Narcissus* (daffodil)
* *Philodendron*
* *Sansevieria trifasciata* (mother-in-law's tongue)
* *Schefflera* (umbrella tree)
* *Spathiphyllum wallisii* (peace lily)
* *Tradescantia* (wandering Jew)
* *Yucca elephantipes* (spineless yucca)
* *Zamioculcas zamiifolia* (ZZ plant)
* *Zantedeschia* (calla lily)

Cleaning

It's true that, if left alone, houseplants will gatherer dust, but this can be prevented. Simply schedule in a few minutes of plant cleaning once a month along with your watering duties. Cleaning houseplants is actually good for their health—if the leaves get too dusty or dirty, the plant won't be able to photosynthesize properly and won't thrive.

TOOLS OF THE TRADE

To make caring for your plants as easy as possible, there are a few essential tools.

* Watering can and mister from Haws (hawswateringcans.com)

* Pruning shears from Felco (felcousa.com)

* Sophie Conran hand trowels from Williams Sonoma (williams-sonoma.com)

* Bamboo support canes from Gardener's Supply Company (gardeners.com)

* Nutscene garden twine from Better Homes & Gardens (bhg.com)

* Terrarium rake from Terrain (shopterrain.com)

CLEANING NEEDS

Your essential tools for the job are a mister and a damp cloth.

* **Cacti** How you clean a cactus depends on its size and type—and how prickly it is! Small cacti can be very prickly, so run Q-tips between the spikes to pick up any dust. For large cacti, either fold up a soft cloth and carefully pass it between the thorns or, better still, put a small sponge or cloth on the end of a stick and use that. A clean, dry paintbrush will also do the trick. Never be tempted to wet a cactus.

* **Ferns & grasses** Regularly misting these plants—which they prefer to watering—cleans them at the same time.

* **Foliage plants** Gently wipe over each leaf with a damp cloth. These plants polish up rather well, so if you want to give the leaves a shine, go back over them with a dry cloth. Don't be tempted to use houseplant polish—a popular pastime in the 1970s—because it can clog the leaf pores.

* **Herbs** Mist regularly to water and clean.

* **Orchids** Gently wipe along the length of their leaves with a damp cloth. The leaves of *Phalaenopsis* (moth orchid) shine up rather well if you go over them afterward with a dry cloth. Leave the flowers alone.

* **Palms** These are surprisingly easy to clean. The quickest way is to drape a damp cloth over each palm, place your hands on either side of each leaf, and gently run the cloths along the length of the leaf from stem to tip.

* **Succulents** Use a clean, dry, soft cloth to run over each leaf gently, from stem to tip.

TIP

Remove dead flowers and leaves the minute you spot them, as these can encourage disease and attract pests.

PLANT DOCTOR

Now that you've decided which plants you want to position where, you should know how to keep them healthy. A house isn't a plant's natural environment and, in short, there is no wind or rain to wash away any problems. This puts plants under stress, making them more susceptible to pests and diseases. Though houseplants are primarily affected by pests, these can lead to diseases, such as mold.

Plant stress is usually caused by easily fixed problems: under- or over-watering, too much or too little light, being too hot or too cold, or even being moved about too frequently (see page 163), but there could be more insidious reasons for your plants starting to look less than their best.

If the usual fixes aren't working, consider that your plant may be suffering from one of the following six common culprits: aphids, mealybugs, scale insects, sciarid flies, red spider mites, or whiteflies. But if you tackle these quickly, your plants will have a good chance of recovery, so make a habit of checking them regularly.

When treating plants with insecticides, always follow the manufacturer's instructions. Unfortunately, if the pest infestation is severe, you may have to cut your losses and dispose of the infected plant before the problem spreads.

Here are the six most common pests that affect houseplants, and how to spot and treat them.

I. Aphids

Appearance Commonly known as plant lice, aphids are usually tiny green flies, but they also come in pink, yellow, or black varieties.
Damage They feed by sucking sap from plants, particularly new tips and leaves, stunting growth. The sticky honeydew they deposit can lead to unsightly sooty molds.
Treatment Use an appropriate insecticide.

2. Mealybugs

Appearance These small, white, spiky insects slightly resemble maggots and feed on or around the leaves. The females cover themselves and their eggs with a sticky white material, making them look cottony.
Damage Like aphids, mealybugs excrete a powdery wax, which can lead to the growth of sooty mold. A serious bout of mealybugs can lead to the plant wilting and the leaves yellowing and dropping.
Treatment Wipe away the mealybugs, as well as the honeydew and sooty mold, with a damp cloth. For a severe infestation, wipe over the affected area with cottonballs or Q-tips dipped in a solution of rubbing alcohol diluted 50/50 with water. Alternatively, spray the insects with an appropriate insecticide.

3. Scale insects

Appearance These flat, brown, hard-shelled insects cling to the stems or the undersides of leaves.
Damage They suck the sap, weakening the plant, and excrete honeydew, which makes the leaves yellow and sticky. Unsightly sooty mold may then follow.
Treatment Pick off the bugs (yes, we know, yuck!) and then treat with an appropriate insecticide. You will probably have to do this several times over several weeks.

TIP
....
You can tackle most common pests initially by wiping the affected parts of your plants with a solution of 50/50 water and dish soap every five days. If it doesn't seem to be having substantial results, you may have to resort to an insecticide.

4. Sciarid flies

Appearance Also called fungus gnats, these tiny black flies with transparent wings can be seen flying around the plant. Their opaque white larvae have black heads.

Damage The flies are harmless, though annoying and unsightly to have in your home, but the larvae of some species can damage the plant by feeding on its new roots.

Treatment Use an appropriate insecticide.

5. Red spider mites

Appearance These tiny red or yellowish-green pests look like specks on fine webbing attached to the undersides of leaves.

Damage The usual sign of an infestation is a pale mottling effect on the top surface of leaves, which then drop off. They can overwhelm the foliage and seriously weaken the plant.

BIOLOGICAL CONTROLS

In his work, Ian uses only biological controls—certain species of insects that prey on problem insects—to treat plant pests because health and safety restrictions prevent the use of pesticides in commercial settings. Biological controls are obviously much better for the environment but they may not be viable in a domestic situation. They tend to be costly and are not usually available in small quantities. Biological controls can also take much longer than standard pesticides to work and they aren't brilliant at dealing with a serious bout of anything. Most people are also likely to be squeamish about introducing insects into their homes to treat other insects.

CHECKING OVER THE GOODS

Inspect your plants carefully before buying and bringing them home. If they show any signs of insect infestation (see pages 166–168), powdery mildew (fuzzy mold), brown spots, holes, or nibbled edges, put them back and seek out healthier specimens.

Treatment Remove infected leaves and spray with an appropriate insecticide—you will have to do this repeatedly because spider mites are persistent. You can also try raising humidity levels by misting the air around the plant or by setting the plant on a tray of gravel filled with water. Spider mites usually attack plants that are already stressed from exposure to hot, dry air, such as in a house with central heat.

6. Whiteflies

Appearance These insects look like tiny, white mothlike creatures.

Damage The adults excrete sticky honeydew, which can lead to sooty mold, while the larvae suck sap from the plant. An infestation can spread rapidly and cause the leaves to turn yellow and fall off.

Treatment Spray with an appropriate insecticide every few days until the flies are gone, but note that only the adult pest is susceptible to insecticides. To treat the larvae, wipe them over with a soapy solution (see Tip on page 166) every three to four days until they are eliminated.

TIP

....

Use the appropriate insecticide for the problem, and only spray it on the affected area, avoiding in particular any unaffected new growth or young leaves to prevent damaging them. Always follow the manufacturer's instructions.

SUPPLIERS

Here are some resources for online companies, nurseries, garden centers, and stores selling essential equipment, cool containers, home accessories, and, of course, plants.

CONTAINERS

Anthropologie (anthropologie.com). Global, bohemian, and very on-trend. Full of colorful, covetable pieces for the home.

A+R (aplusrstore.com). Simple, elegant containers for a sleek minimalist aesthetic.

Cost Plus World Market (worldmarket.com). A variety of hanging, geometric, and apothecary terrarium containers, plus accessories.

Crate & Barrel (crateandbarrel.com). Contemporary home decor with fantastic large planters and baskets, elegant ceramic and glass containers, and shelving for creative displays.

Eleanor Bolton (eleanorbolton.com). Young jewelry designer who is almost single-handedly responsible for the revival of hanging macramé plant holders, except hers are brilliantly updated in a range of monochromes and neons.

Etsy (etsy.com). All about craft, quirkiness, individuality, and independence. A great source for unusual planters and containers from small companies and creatives.

Gardener's Supply Company (gardeners.com). A great resource for any plantsperson, with basics like tools and soil, but also high-style items, such as magnetic succulent pots for the fridge and gorgeous copper hanging terrariums.

H & M Home (hm.com). Brilliantly affordable and on-trend. Our favorite source for metallic pots and quick-update home accessories.

Home Depot (homedepot.com). Go-to garden center with a wide array of planter urns, hanging planters, window boxes, and tools and houseplants to get any home going green.

Houzz (houzz.com). A large selection of timeless rustic and modern containers, from wooden plant theaters to cowboy boot planters.

IKEA (ikea.com). Affordable, accessible, and comprehensive selection of planters, plus plants to put in them.

Jonathan Adler (jonathanadler.com). An interior design store offering a wide range of distinctive, occasionally surreal vessels, a testament to its founder's early career as a potter.

Joss & Main (jossandmain.com). A nice selection of planter pots, baskets, and trays that will set the right mood for your houseplant displays, whether you're after a dose of kitsch or understated simplicity.

Lowe's (lowes.com). Garden center with a wide range of planters, plant stands, and window boxes, plus a hearty selection of houseplants.

Lumens (lumens.com). A handsome assortment of monochrome planters in classic as well as unexpected shapes for a decor statement that is refined and modern.

Neo-utility (neo-utility.com). Quirky contemporary upside-down hanging planters from Boskke, stylish watering cans from XALA, and other creative containers from a well-curated selection of designers.

Novica (novica.com). National Geographic's socially conscious global marketplace, showcasing handmade crafts from international artisans, including vibrant hand-painted planters, fantastic woven basketry, and carved coconut hanging pots.

Pier 1 Imports (pier1.com). Eclectic home decor, from terrarium-friendly lanterns to whimsical wall planters.

Terrain (shopterrain.com). Anthropologie's boho-chic home and garden brand, with planters in tapered birch and brushed silver, terrarium containers with tools and accessories, and grow kits for the DIY-inclined. They also sell prestyled bulbs, air plants, and hanging ferns for an instant decor upgrade.

Tuscan Imports (tuscanimports.com). Traditional planters, vases, and urns made from authentic Italian terracotta. A wonderful choice for bringing the feeling of a rustic Tuscan garden into the home.

Uncommon Goods (uncommongoods.com). Rare and adorable plant containers and accessories, including seed kits, grow-lamp planters, and eco-friendly fish tanks for a mini aquaponics garden.

Urban Outfitters (urbanoutfitters.com). Recently introduced a well-edited range of beautiful terrariums and metal planters.

Vitra (vitra.com). Sells beautiful twentieth-century design classics as well as new pieces by twenty-first-century names. Amazing accessories that can be used as unusual planters, including the understated Uten.Silo wall rack, the Toolbox caddy, and the Corniche Shelves for individual displays.

Wayfair (wayfair.com). Home furnishing company hosting a charming collection of wooden and metal plant stands and ingenious planters of nearly every shape, material, and size.

West Elm (westelm.com). A great selection of unusual containers and cool plant stands, including quirky designs by Brighton-based ceramicist Atelier Stella.

PLANTS

Adams & Son Gardens (adamsandsongardens.com). Family-owned Chicago shop boasting a luscious gallery of trailing plants and large architectural varieties.

Annie's Annuals (anniesannuals.com). Massive online plant retailer out of Richmond, CA, with a dazzling selection of plants listed on its website.

Artemisia (collagewithnature.com). Quaint Portland terrarium workshop specializing in DIY, selling all the fixings alongside their premade pieces.

Flora Grubb (floragrubb.com) San Francisco nursery with a variety of architectural houseplants, and a plethora of succulents, air plants, and chic modern containers. Certainly worth a visit for its adjoining cafe and decor alone.

Foliage Paradise (paradiseplantsny.com). NYC plant shop with an impressive selection of houseplants, orchids, bromeliads, air plants, succulents, and cacti. Ships within the state and to surrounding areas.

Forestfarm (forestfarm.com). An online retailer out of Williams, OR, great for ferns, palms, and pines.

Garden Heights Nursery (gardenheights.com). One-stop garden shop in St. Louis, MO, with everything from plants to tools to pots and garden decor.

Gethsemane Garden Center (gethsemanegardens. com). This forty-year-old, family-owned and -operated Chicago shop covers all your indoor planting needs, from bonsai to cacti, not to mention terrarium workshops and local delivery.

Paxton Gate (paxtongate.com). Specializes in natural oddities to fill your home with a magical touch. A great resource for DIY and premade pieces, and a must-see for tourists in San Francisco and Portland.

Pistils Nursery (pistilsnursery.com). Portland shop selling plants, containers, and decor online, with workshops in terrariums, kokedama, and staghorn-fern mounting.

Portland Nursery (portlandnursery.com). Accessible garden center has all the houseplants, tools, and containers you need at their three Portland locations.

Rolling Greens (rollinggreensnursery.com). Culver City, CA, location boasting eight greenhouses that cover four terraced levels and topiaries, exotic orchids, exterior plants, cacti, succulents, and foliage.

The Sill (thesill.com). NYC plant shop with an impressive variety of houseplants available for local and nationwide delivery, and a name that's a nod to indoor gardening's prime real estate.

Sky Nursery (skynursery.com). Shoreline, WA, nursery on the outskirts of Seattle. An amazing selection of pots and indoor plants.

Succulence (thesucculence.com). San Francisco treasure with hearty plants from classic to trendy, with workshops in moss walls, vertical gardening, terrariums, and aeriums.

Sunset Nursery (sunsetblvdnursery.com). Los Angeles nursery with a huge selection of houseplants from desert to tropical.

University Gardens (university-gardens.com). St. Louis, MO, nursery selling a large, unique selection of houseplants with a designer on staff to help with your vision.

Verdant Matter (verdantmatter.blogspot. com). Stylish Chicago plant boutique specializing in local, handmade, and eco-friendly designs and products, including houseplants and planters, ceramic goods, accessories, and gifts.

TOOLS

Better Homes & Gardens (bhg.com). Online store with a wealth of tools and containers, even containers for your tools. They also make selection easier with the expertise of their "Editor's Picks."

Felco (felcousa.com). Your go-to for every type and variety of pruning shears.

Garden Tool Co. (gardentoolcompany.com) Top-of-the-line online retailer for gardening tools from brands including Felco, Sneeboer, and Haws. They even carry garden tools in kids' sizes for the budding gardener in your family.

Niwaki (niwaki.com). Utterly beautiful gardening tools from Japan. Function and form at its very best.

Williams Sonoma (williams-sonoma.com). An extensive online shop as well as brick-and-mortar stores nationwide, hosting a stylish set of Burgon & Ball garden tools from interior designer Sophie Conran as well as neat DIY herb seed kits, vertical garden walls, and more for indoor and outdoor gardeners.

INDEX

INDEX

171

weldon**owen**

Published in North America
by Weldon Owen
1045 Sansome Street
San Francisco, CA 94111
www.weldonowen.com

Weldon Owen is a division of
Bonnier Publishing USA.

This edition published in 2017.

First published in Great Britain
in 2017 by Mitchell Beazley,
a division of Octopus Publishing Group Ltd.

Copyright © Octopus Publishing Group
Limited 2017

Kara O'Reilly and Ian Drummond assert
their moral right to be identified as the
authors of this work.

ISBN 978-1-68188-281-9

Library of Congress Cataloging in
Publication data is available.

10 9 8 7 6 5 4 3 2
2017 2018 2019 2020 2021

Printed and bound in China.

PICTURE CREDITS

Key: a above; b below; c center; l left; r right

123RF Kari Klaustermeier 121bcl; **Alamy** Andrea Jones 95r; D Hurst 107al; Flavia Raddavero/Image Broker 155bcr; John Swithinbank 167ar; Nigel Cattlin 167bl & br; Profimedia.cz 143bl; Steffen Hauser/ botanikfoto 154al; Tashphotography/ Stockimo 79ar; Tim Gainey 79bcr; Vario Images 78ar; Wildlife 130ar; **Camera Press** Flora 79bl; **Dorling Kindersley** 131ar; Sian Irvine 95bcl; Verity Welstead 154br; **Dreamstime.com** Adaychou 131acl; Anna Chelnokova 95bl; Blackslide 95bcr; Dreammasterphotographer 121br; Ileana Marcela Bosogea-Tudor 94al; irabel8 155bl; Joloei 107bl; Karidesign 131al; Kateryna Potrokhova 107ar; Llepet 120bl; Marius Craciun 78br; Nmorozova 154ar; Noppanun Kunjai 155br; Panya Chitmedha

107bcl; Sdbower 142ar; Srugina 155bcl; **Fotolia** brhlena 131acr; Dragan Nikolic 143br; Eric Isselée 143bcl; L Bouvier 131bl; Melica 121acr; Morgenstjerne 131bcr; prwstd 131br; vencav 79acl; **GAP Photos** Clive Nichols/design Clare Matthews 107acr, 143acl, 155acr; Friedrich Strauss 120ar, 130br; Inna Karpova 79bcl; John Glover 95al; Juliette Wade 95acr, 106al, 142bl; Thomas Alamy 143acr, Visions 94ar & bl, 121acl & ar, 130bl, 154bl, 155al; **Garden World Images** Andrea Jones 143ar; Flora Press 94br; Floramedia 78bl, 79br, 121al, 142br, 143al, 155acl; **Getty Images** DEA/C Dani 79acr, G Cigolini 106br; **istockphoto. com** andypantz 167al; **living4media** Cecilia Möller 120br; **Loupe Images** CICO Books Ltd 142al; **Nature Picture Library** Nick Upton 167cr; **Octopus Publishing Group** Giulia Hetherington 120al; **Science Photo Library** Ron Chapman 107br; **Shutterstock** Amawasri Pakdara 143bcr; Elena Elisseeva 106ar; irabel8 155acr; Kittibowornphatnon 95acl; lynea 121bl; Madlen 95br; Santia 167cl; Sergiu Birca 106bl; wasanajai 107acl; **The Garden Collection** Flora Press 131bcl/ Carolinen Bureck 130al, Nova Photo Graphik 78al, 79al.

Pages 10–11: 10al storage tins © Rockett St George; roots glass plant pot 10ac © Nude Living; 10ar succulents © 4ᵗʰ Floor; 10cl Madam Stoltz planters © Out There Interiors; 10cc Bloomingville planters © Out There Interiors; 10cr Lacroix fabric © Designers Guild; 10bl jungle wallpaper © Cole & Son; Nordal planting scheme 10bc © Out There Interiors; 10br Tarovine wallpaper and fabric © House of Hackney; 11al cacti © Darkroom; 11ac restaurant © Rawduck; 11ar terrariums © Rockett St George; 11cl herb vases © Cox & Cox; 11cc lookbook © Conran; 11cr *Monstera deliciosa* © Habitat; 11bl terrariums © Graham & Green; 11bc pillow © House of Hackney; 11br hanging planters © MiaFleur.

Pages 48–49: All images supplied by Shutterstock apart from 48cc *Monstera deliciosa* © Joy of Plants; 48ar Sunflowers © McQueens; 49bl Vanda Orchids catwalk © Kinder Aggugini, London Fashion Week; 49bc A herb table © James Royall; 49al Paul Smith © Paul Smith.

THANKS & DEDICATIONS

Our thanks to Jean Egbunike, without whom this book would never have come to be.

To the shoot team: Nick Pope, for his unfailingly good and gorgeous photography; Elkie Brown, for her fabulous styling and boundless energy; and the members of the Indoor Garden Design team, with special thanks to Deanne.

To the owners of all the lovely locations who were kind enough to let us invade their homes and who were so welcoming on the shoot days: Linda, Fintan, Finn, and Nansai Mooney; Liliana, Mario, Emilia, Luca, and Nico; Joe, Bex, Tilda, and Beth; Lindsay, Matt, and Olive; Maria, Enzo, Luca, Gabriela, and Natalia; Salia and last, but not least, Kally.

The team at Octopus for their commitment to the cause: Alison Starling, Polly Poulter, and Jonathan Christie.

From Kara: With love to: Mark, Ailbe, and Ned—you are my world; Dad and Cas for their invaluable support during the writing process—both practical and emotional; Mum for her good taste—which, I suspect, got me into interiors in the first place.

From Ian: To my mum, Peggy, and sister, Lisa, for their love and support. Mum, thank you for making that phone call 28 years ago. Also thanks to Allan, for the days and late nights to get this completed and making another dream come true.

KARA O'REILLY

Kara is an experienced and prolific writer and editor of lifestyle and interior design features. She has worked on and contributed to some of the most influential style magazines and newspapers on the market, including *Style* at the *Sunday Times*, *Elle Decoration*, and *Livingetc*. Kara is currently Interiors Editor at luxury lifestyle magazine *The Resident*.

IAN DRUMMOND

Ian is Creative Director of Indoor Garden Design. A true north-London boy, Ian uses garden and horticultural design to express his understanding of city living. He has worked on installations for the Barbican Art Gallery and St Pancras Station in London, as well as scooping up an impressive array of medals at the RHS Chelsea Flower Show. Ian's work mainly focuses on creative projects—film premieres, fashion shows, and charity functions, including The BAFTAs and the annual Sir Elton John AIDS Foundation's White Tie & Tiara Ball. He is devoted to his craft, and is passionate about bringing the garden into the heart of the home. Ian is also Ambassador of eFIG (European Federation of Interior Landscape Groups) and an RHS committee member.